Do More *Now*

GET BETTER LATER

STOP being your own worst enemy and **START** making money

JOHN WETMORE

© 2024 2MARKET MEDIA

ISBN 979-8-218-45859-1

All rights reserved. No portion of this book may be reproduced, stored in a retrieval system, or transmitted in any form or by any means - electronic, mechanical, photocopy, recording, scanning, or other - except for brief quotations in critical reviews or articles, without the prior written permission of the publisher.

Published by 2MARKET MEDIA with John Wetmore.

Contents

Dedication v

Introduction vii

Chapter One: My Minimum Wage Age 1

Chapter Two: Winning And Losing It All 17

Chapter Three: No Sure Thing In Insurance 29

Chapter Four: Seventeen, Or The Number
    That Changed My Life 45

Chapter Five: Discipline 65

Chapter Six: Ownership 93

Chapter Seven: Mistakes 115

Chapter Eight: Obsession 123

Chapter Nine: Resilience 141

Chapter Ten: Expectations 159

Chapter Eleven: Silk Pajamas 183

The Tools You Need 201

Acknowledgements 207

Dedication

Thanks to my wife, Stephanie Wetmore, for supporting me every step of the way through this crazy journey. Through all the ups and downs of life, nobody has had more faith in me, believing that I can be great and accomplish more!

Introduction

One thing you need to know about me is that I'm a mess. I grew up dirt-poor in the projects. I got rich quick off subprime mortgages and lost it all in the crash. I got my house taken away and went bankrupt. I went through a divorce, and for years, I self-medicated on a dangerous cocktail of antidepressants and alcohol.

Why am I telling you this? Well, I'm pretty sure you aren't perfect either. And if *I've* managed to turn things around and make a success out of myself, then it's a damn certainty that you can too.

Today, I'm a managing partner at one of the largest life insurance companies in the world: Integrity Marketing Group, which acquired my agency, Family First Life Agent Force, in 2020. My agency issued $200 million in premiums in 2023. My team averages $1,500 per life insurance policy, and dozens of my agents clear $500,000 a year in personal sales alone.

I went from not knowing if I was going to be able to put food on the table, to providing a life and home for my children that I never dreamed of, as well as giving opportunities to agents I meet and train all over the country. Some days, I'm still shocked by how far I've come. But it happened to me. And I want you to believe that it can happen to you too.

How did I make the change? People call me John "Do More" Wetmore for a reason. It's a mantra I live by. I've made a handy acronym to expand on my principles for success because, well, everyone loves an acronym:

DISCIPLINE
OWNERSHIP

MISTAKES
OBSESSION
RESILIENCE
EXPECTATIONS

In the chapters of this book, I'll go through each of these principles, and the hope is that you are convinced enough to adopt them. You'll notice I write *principles for success* instead of *secrets to success*. These aren't secrets. There's no snake oil on sale here. But this system worked for me.

My goal is to show you that in order to make it to the top of any field, you don't have to be an expert first. You just have to work hard. You'll learn as you go along. Your mistakes—and the lessons you draw from them—will guide you.

In this book, I'll share personal failures and successes, explaining how I learned, little by little, to trust my instincts—and how doing so led me to believe in and follow my guiding principle: learn by doing. Then I'll walk you through my method and show you exactly how to get better at sales (or whatever work you do) by diving in and learning from your mistakes.

I set out to get rich, but along the way, I realized that helping others get rich was by far the most satisfying part of that journey. It's why I've written this book. Hopefully, I can play a small part in your success story.

CHAPTER ONE
MY MINIMUM WAGE AGE

L ife insurance is not a sexy business. Ask a classroom full of elementary school students what they want to be when they grow up, and you're not going to find any insurance salespeople among the future astronauts, TikTok influencers, and pop stars.

The first time a buddy asked me if I wanted to get into insurance, I laughed and said, "No thanks." Who would want to call up random people to remind them that one day they're going to die, and then hound them for money? You're just asking to get hung up on or yelled at.

But then I thought to myself: *wait a second*. You hate your accounting job. You're broke and coming off bankruptcy because your previous job in mortgages went south. Your boss sucks. What's the harm in trying?

And I'm so glad I did; it changed my life. But the transformation didn't happen immediately.

Life insurance is easy to get into. You could roll out of bed tomorrow and say, "I want to be an insurance guy," and basically be one. There's a test, but it only costs two hundred dollars, and my dog could pass it. Once you have your license and put your resume out there, thousands of people will call you offering work. Getting into the business is not the issue. It's staying in it.

The industry has a ridiculous turnover rate. Companies absolutely whore themselves out to agents because the vast majority don't make it. In the eyes of the consumer, an insurance guy is a douchebag trying to sell you something you don't want to think about. Navigating calls and sales can be a nightmare when you're just getting abuse and rejection hurled at you over the phone. It's a tough uphill climb at the beginning.

That was the case for me. I wasn't born to be an insurance guy. It's not in my blood, and I didn't have parents or uncles or cousins in the business to show me the ropes. I had to figure it out myself. So, I did what made the most sense to me: I studied like hell. I wanted to know and understand everything about the field in order to be good at it and get myself on the track to financial freedom instead of living paycheck to paycheck.

I didn't want to make any mistakes. But that meant I worked slowly and cautiously. And sure, I was learning, but I was only getting average results. After a few years, I knew I had to do something different if I wanted to excel. So, I decided to live by a new guiding philosophy. *Do More Now* and *Get Better Later.*

I figured out a way to not just perform, but succeed and thrive in my field, and I want to share it all with you. Because what I have learned is that I get the most professional satisfaction from helping others succeed and thrive right alongside me.

I was happy when I made my first $100,000 from selling insurance. But I was over the damn moon when I started paying my staff six-figure salaries. I think it brings me so much pleasure because I know what it's like to not have much.

I was a kid from the hood who clawed my way to financial stability before losing it all in the 2007 financial crisis, but then I got it all back—and way more—by getting into life insurance and choosing to make mistakes.

I'm not an expert. I'm not a genius. And I'm not a guru, I'm just a guy who worked really hard, consistently and didn't quit.

I was thirty-five when I got into the industry—I was broke, bankrupt, and fighting my way out of a dark depression. I sucked for two years, and I quit twice. I did not come into this as a guy who was a number-one producer out of the gate. But I became that. I'm here to show you that if I could do it, you can do it too.

My method is simple. You don't have to be the best at what you do. You don't have to be phenomenal at sales. You don't have to be the most articulate person in the world. And you don't have to have an encyclopedic understanding of the field. I tried that.

I thought I needed to know everything about life insurance to be good at it, so for two years, I spent more energy studying than selling. But then I realized I was earning a lot less than some of my colleagues who weren't the brightest bulbs, the best talkers, or the most knowledgeable people in the industry. So, I decided to stop being a student, and I dove into the work, making mistakes and learning from them along the way.

And I was just me: a normal guy who tells it like it is. No frills. No lies. That's how I made it to the top. I had to bust my ass to get good at selling insurance, and I had to sacrifice a lot. But it worked. And it's built me a ridiculous life.

Let me start from the beginning. I was born and raised in Lynn, Massachusetts. To this day, when I tell people that, some people sing back, "Lynn, Lynn, the city of sin?" repeating my hometown's infamous slogan. Lynn has long been a blue-collar, industrial city with a reputation for vice and crime; it was a hub for prostitution and liquor during Prohibition. By the time I was born there, it was the proper hood. I'm not talking about Compton levels, but it was still rough. It was a melting pot of communities, of single moms on welfare and food stamps—like mine—and a bunch of us hoodrats, running around and hustling. From the time I was a kid, I was always looking to make a buck or two. I sold candy to my classmates at recess. Later, I sold Christmas trees out of our living room.

My mom had me when she was eighteen, and because she made more money on welfare than a job, she stayed on it. It allowed her to go to school while taking care of my little brother and me. My dad, a machinist who was in and out of the picture—more often out than in—wasn't a huge help.

From the start, my mom's goal was to get my brother and me out of the projects. She worried about me especially: I stayed out of trouble, but I flirted with it a whole lot. From a young age, I was always near drugs and booze. I didn't partake too much, aside from the occasional joint at the convenience store or wine cooler that I stole from my mom's fridge. But the more my friends got involved, the harder my mom fought to get me away from them. One of the first things she did when she got her first job was to enroll me at a small, local Catholic school to prevent me from going to public school with all my friends.

I hated it. I hated my stupid blue-and-yellow uniform, I hated wearing a tie, and I was pissed to be separated from my friends. I did everything I could to get kicked out: I skipped class, I didn't do my homework, I interrupted my teachers, talking through their lessons. I racked up demerits thinking they were my ticket out: enough of those bad boys and the school would have to expel me. But just when I thought I was close, the principal called me in and told me a new rule applied to me: each time I acted out, I'd get a demerit taken away from my stash. It was simple. I wasn't getting out of school. And I didn't. I was there through eighth grade.

It was the same song and dance for high school. I desperately wanted to go to public school with all my friends, but my mom enrolled me at a technical school for ninth grade and then moved us out of Lynn altogether to another city in Massachusetts. To me, Beverly was a preppie nightmare. My mom had gotten a computer programming job on a community college campus there, always working hard to give my brother and me a better life. But I didn't get it at the time. I was just mad about being surrounded by teens I had nothing in common with. I wanted to be a rapper. They wore upturned collars. I hopped on the train back to Lynn whenever I could.

But eventually, I settled in. I met a girl in Beverly that I liked: Jamie. And then everything changed. A few weeks after we started dating, Jamie got pregnant. I was going to be a dad, and I was only sixteen.

To be honest, I was stoked. I love kids. I always have. I was the oldest out of all my cousins and often took care of kids at family get-togethers, and I had fun doing it. But now, for the first time in my life, I also had to provide. I had to make money. I had to get a job.

I found one at the local Little Caesars. Soon enough, I was kneading dough, firing up ovens, and working the register. While I was in high school, I would leave early on work release and go in on weekends, so I probably put in thirty to forty hours a week. After high school, I went straight into seventy-hour weeks.

It was hard work, but I liked it a lot more than sitting in class. I was getting paid, and I was good at the job. I climbed the ranks quickly, and soon enough, I was running shifts —and then the whole shop. My boss trusted me. I was there. I didn't miss work. I didn't bitch. I was super consistent. If you dropped me in a Little Caesars today, I bet you I could still run the place even though it's been twenty-something years. I got a taste of what it was like to be valued and rewarded for good work.

I graduated high school, married my girlfriend, and kept busting my ass at the pizza joint. I didn't complain, but seventy-plus hours at minimum wage wasn't the dream. Often, in the morning when I left our apartment for Little Caesars, I ran into our neighbor coming home from work. He worked the night shift at a food distribution warehouse. One day, he told me I should try it out: the gig was eighteen dollars an hour plus overtime. I didn't need to do any serious kind of math to see that that was the better deal. I moved on to the warehouse.

My job was to load food orders onto pallets and into trucks for distribution to restaurants throughout the city. It was super important to build a good, sturdy base; otherwise, your pallet could tip over as you navigated the pallet jack through the aisles. The trick to the whole thing was making sure you placed everything in the right order with the driver's unloading process top of mind. If the first restaurant on the route ordered one pack of chili flakes, and you stuck that behind eight boxes of canned tomatoes, you'd be slowing the whole process down—and the driver would certainly let you and your supervisor know about it.

We were encouraged to work quickly; everything was timed. You'd clock in and clock out for each order, and your efficiency was graded. Anything less than 85% and you'd hear about it.

I watched a lot of guys in the warehouse race to finish building their pallets and load them up. But their pallets weren't sturdy and would topple over; or they were illogically assembled, so they'd screw up the orders.

I didn't rush. I spent more time upfront, carefully making my pallets; then I would look at the whole order and figure out a game plan for loading the food. It looked like I was working slowly, but I was the most efficient guy in the warehouse. I was making and loading the most pallets in a record amount of time.

My manager didn't get it at first. He'd yell, "What are you doing? Hurry up, we've got shit to do!" And I'd shoot back, "Go look at my scores, dude. I'm like number one in the warehouse right now. Leave me alone."

Once he confirmed how efficient I was, he did leave me alone. And I eventually became known for building the best pallets, in the fastest times, even though it appeared I wasn't. This would be a common theme in my future career, and I learned a ton from this experience that I still apply to this day.

At Little Caesars, I learned the value of good, hard work. At the warehouse, I learned to trust my gut. I was most efficient working at my own rhythm and speed and in my own style. I didn't need anyone to micromanage me. I do a good job on my own. You don't have to bug me. I'm competitive, so I'll strive to be first, but I'll do it my way.

I liked working at the warehouse, but I couldn't do it forever. One day, I looked around and saw my coworkers—guys in their forties and fifties with sore backs and messed-up elbows—still loading boxes twenty or thirty years into the job. For blue-collar work, it paid well: you could make fifty or sixty grand a year, which was a lot in the late '90s and early 2000s. It was good money, but it took a toll on your body. One common theme I noticed was that the entire career goal of the night shift guys was to get on the day shift. That was it. Work 7:00 a.m. through 4:00 p.m. at the warehouse instead of 6:00 p.m. through 4:00 a.m. The day shift was technically easier work because they didn't have to pick orders; they just restocked full pallets of the stuff we picked at night. So less manual labor, but that was it for dreams.

I was in my early twenties, and as I looked around the warehouse, I saw my future. And I decided, "Nope." That wasn't for me. I wasn't a lifer. So, I decided it was time to go to college and get a degree.

At twenty-two, I walked into the same community college my mom had attended to get her programming degree, and I stared at a board covered in little sheets of yellow, green, and blue paper with the names of each major printed on them.

A counselor approached me. "What do you want to do?" she asked. "I have no idea," I replied. "Well, what are you good at?" she asked instead. I told her I was good at math. "Then you should do accounting," she said. I enrolled right then and there, and to this day, I blame her for becoming an accountant.

For the next two years, I worked at the warehouse at night, went home, picked up my daughter Shailey, took her to daycare, and then headed off to college, attending classes full-time during the day.

I ran on fumes during that time, catching just a couple hours of sleep a night and topping up with catnaps in my car parked in a lot around the corner from my kid's daycare before drop-off.

After two years of that schedule, I finally got my first "adult job," an accounting internship that my stepdad hooked me up with. I think it paid ten dollars an hour. My job was to reconcile state grant money on spreadsheets all day. Boring as hell, but boy would that spreadsheet training come in handy for my future insurance days.

It was great to finally have a job where I could sit down in an office and be home by late afternoon. After I received my associate degree, I got a job with the city of New Hampshire. But it wasn't for me—I'm not a guy who wears khakis and chit-chats by the watercooler with people I have nothing in common with. I didn't like the environment. On top of that, the pay cut was brutal. I was only making thirty grand a year, and now I had two kids. I wanted—and needed—more.

I've always known I'm not the kind of person who'll invent anything earth-shattering or cure a disease. But I always figure out how to get a little something extra. I've always had hustle in me, from the time I was selling candy at recess back in Lynn.

When my uncle, a cop who'd started a side hustle selling mortgages, suggested I give mortgages a whirl, I agreed. And that's when I finally started making real money.

CHAPTER TWO
WINNING AND LOSING IT ALL

The mortgage game was stupid easy to get into. It was 2005, and you didn't need a license. I took a class, got a certificate, and started selling mortgages on the side. We'd just moved to Georgia—where I'd taken up another accounting job—and was just about to finish my bachelor's, which I'd been working towards at night for the last two years.

I refinanced my coworkers because interest rates were so low. I didn't need to know anybody, I didn't need to network, and I made a couple grand every time.

One of my coworkers' brothers was an *investor*. I later found out everyone was an investor in 2005–2006 when they were handing out 100% investment loans with no proof of income. I once closed four loans for this dude in one day with zero proof of income.

Around that time, I left my work desk fifteen minutes early to hit the bathroom before my lunch break started. When I returned, my boss started giving me an earful. It all just came to a head at that moment. I'd had to eat shit just to crawl toward a best-case-scenario of an eighty thousand dollars salary in thirty years' time. Screw that. I told my boss where to shove it and walked out that day to start a mortgage career from my basement.

The mortgage industry turbo-charged my inner hustler. I was getting paid a 50% commission of several thousands of dollars for each loan, and the broker that had trained me was keeping the other 50%. Other than the initial training, they weren't really offering a ton of value, and after a couple web searches, I learned that *I* could be a broker for a one-hundred-dollar application fee to the state. This was before the subprime mortgage crash and long before today's regulations.

I went and applied, then started my company. What would I name it? "Auburn Mortgage," after the college of my favorite athlete, Bo Jackson. My son, Maddox, actually wears the number thirty-four to this day, in honor of Bo who wore it for the Oakland Raiders.

So, on March 10, 2006, I officially owned my first company. My strategy was simple: I hired a bunch of the people I'd been in class with and let them keep 75% of the sale, instead of the 50% brokers usually allowed. And the money just rolled in. I had no idea what I was doing, but I saw people all around me get rich quick and thought, *if they can do it, I can do it. Just let me figure this out.*

We sold subprime loans, first from my basement and then from an office we rented. It was a wild time: everyone was investing, and no one had a clue what they were doing. You'd go to a bank, you'd get a loan, they'd give you cash for all of it—no questions asked—and bam, you had a house. I bought a big house I couldn't afford—in addition to the house we lived in. All I had to show were my bank statements, and they only looked at deposits, not withdrawals. If it had all kept going just a little bit longer, I would have made six figures. But then the market crashed, and hundreds of lenders went out of business essentially overnight. They froze funding on all the loans we had pending.

I lost everything in one day. By 2008, I'd had my two houses foreclosed, I lost my truck, I filed for bankruptcy, and I got divorced. I had four kids and no job to provide for them. I moved into a pay-by-night motel crawling with roaches. I drank to numb the depression that had sunk its claws into me. I was on Lexapro. Taken together, the booze and the antidepressants made everything worse. Every day, I applied to dozens of jobs in accounting or warehouses—the only things I knew to do—but nothing. No one was hiring. Those were the darkest times of my life.

This was also when I met Stephanie. One of the earliest memories I have is of her bringing Thanksgiving Day leftovers from her mom's house to me at that roach-infested motel. We had just met, and she definitely wasn't ready to introduce me to her parents with all the baggage I had, but I knew this girl was the one.

She was on a mission to get me off the Lexapro and back on my feet. Hell, she even helped me pay my child support at times when I came up short. We've now been married for 14 years, and she has been a rock for me through my many stupid decisions in life; one day, I'll probably write a separate book about all of that.

By some miracle, I clinched a job at a call center. It was the only place for miles hiring; I stood in a line with thousands of people—from blue-collar workers to executives in crisp suits—for hours just to get an interview.

They actually bussed us in from a parking lot a few miles away; that many people were there looking for any kind of work. I got the job and was paid ten dollars an hour to take inbound customer service calls for AT&T cell phone customers, again working a night shift: 6:00 p.m.–3:00 a.m.

I took a second job in the day, making eight dollars an hour doing grunt work at a tax company. Finally, several months later, I got an accounting job with a spa business. I asked for thirty-five grand, they said how about forty grand, and I immediately said yes, not knowing that the company was in bankruptcy, and that the next four years would be a wild, stressful ride—not to mention an hour-and-a-half commute at

5:30 a.m. every day with an average two hours back in Atlanta traffic.

But things were starting to look up. I had steady work, and by then, I'd moved in with Stephanie. I don't know how I would have gotten back on my feet without her. But after a couple years, I started to feel the old itch. I hated my accounting job, and I wanted something more exciting that earned more. I needed to provide for my kids. I'd been given a small taste of a decent quality of life before the crash, and I wanted to get that back.

I decided to get into mortgage protection insurance as a part-time job. It was 2010, Stephanie and I had just gotten married, the economy had recovered somewhat. I was familiar with mortgages, so I thought it might be a good fit. I got my insurance license, and then, one afternoon, I settled in Steph's basement and dialed, dialed, dialed. I made maybe thirty calls that day. Everyone told me to fuck off or hung up on me. And I thought, *nah, I'm not doing this.* I shelved the idea and went back to accounting.

Two years later, in the spring of 2012, I got a Facebook message from a guy I'd hired during my mortgage days. Jeremy had been a good friend, but we hadn't spoken since the crash—he'd also gone through some hard times, and I felt somewhat responsible for getting him into that mess. But here he was, writing: *Hey, what are you up to? I'm sure you hate your job. I've got something you might be good at.*

I called him. Jeremy told me he was working in insurance and offered to get me in. I laughed and told him, "No way." But he invited me to meet him for a drink at a sports bar to talk it over anyway. And there, after a few hours, he convinced me. He explained how insurance wasn't so different from the mortgage business; the commission structure and concept were very similar. I decided to give it another try.

I was a different guy by then. With Steph's help, I'd pulled myself out of my depression, and I felt up to the challenge. I sat with Jeremy on his back patio, and we called leads. I thought, *if Jeremy can do it, I can do it too.* And it worked. People listened, and I sold insurance. I got my confidence back and decided to take this side hustle to a new level. I started going to trainings and meeting people, and I saw how much money was in this field.

I was inspired: some people were making crazy money, and they were dipshits. I thought, *I'm just one of them. I'm just a regular guy. If that fool can do it, so can I.*

That first year, I made sixty grand working part-time. It gave me the confidence to let go of the accounting job and go all in.

My first year full-time, I cracked one hundred grand. But that was nothing compared to the high earners of the company, and I was still living paycheck to paycheck. I had five kids to take care of now—Steph and I had a baby of our own. It was stressful. And I didn't feel confident about work. I wasn't excelling. I was cautious. I struggled to communicate with clients, and I wasn't great at recruiting. I was still getting kicked out of houses, and although the end of the year didn't look bad, day to day, week to week, I was super inconsistent. If a client canceled, I might not have gotten paid that week, which frustrated me. I didn't really know how to sell. I thought I had to *learn* to do it before I could do it properly, so I spent a lot of time watching other guys and studying. But I was falling behind.

Then one day, I got a letter at my office. It was a notice informing me that I had to start paying one thousand dollars in alimony each month. I'd deferred for five years as part of my divorce because at the time, I'd been earning little or nothing.

And sure, I was making money now, but that one thousand a month was going to hurt. I lost my shit. I shouted and kicked my desk, then immediately felt worse because I didn't want to be angry about paying more money for my kids.

My buddy Mike Killimett noticed I was off and asked what was up, so I told him.

"Can I ask you something?" he responded.

"Sure," I said.

"Why are you getting this upset over an amount you could earn by writing one extra application a month?"

Mike had a way of getting the point across in a simple manner that you couldn't argue with. He became my greatest mentor to date.

It was a wake-up call. I decided that I never again wanted to be in a position where I was anxious about money when it came to providing for my kids. Never again would I worry about one thousand dollars.

I'd noticed how the high earners in the company made significantly more calls than me. They took on more leads and scheduled more appointments. I'd been holding off until I got better. But I decided to not waste time anymore. I thought, *fuck it; what if I just start doing more? I'll get better later.*

I committed to taking on thirty in-home presentation appointments a week, which came out to 120 a month, and 1,500 a year. And I thought, if I have 1,500 appointments a year and only one thousand of those show up, and I only close twenty-five percent of them, I'll make $250,000. And that was my new strategy. I no longer cared about being good. I knew I sucked, but if I just sucked way more often than everyone else sucked, I could make way more money than them.

That year, 2015, I ended up making $460,000. My whole world changed. I was raking in significantly higher sums than I had at the peak of my mortgage days. I became one of the top producers in the company and started training and hiring people. I helped build the agency up, teaching this very simple concept over and over again: it's okay to suck—just suck more until you get better, and print money along the way. The agency became big enough to be acquired in 2020. Today I'm a Managing Partner. I've never worried about providing for my family again.

I love the insurance industry. I've met so many cool people. I'm honored to get to teach, train, and speak to people who look up to me. And that's why I'm writing this book. If a shit show like me could get here, you absolutely can too. My story proves that it's all about being consistent, not quitting, and learning from your mistakes.

Most people don't kill it in this industry from day one. But it's worth the fight. I'll show you how to do it.

CHAPTER THREE
NO SURE THING IN INSURANCE

What is life insurance? Put plainly, if you have life insurance, when you die, your family gets a check. It's not that deep. There are intricacies, but at its core, in return for a small monthly fee, when your time comes, the life insurance company has to cough up a big lump sum for your family or whoever the beneficiary may be.

Now, why life insurance? Well, from my standpoint, it's not a bad thing to do for a living. You are providing families with a safety net, security, and reassurance when a really, really bad day comes. And those bad days are coming for all of us; it's just a matter of time.

In the case of people getting sick, sometimes you can see that bad day coming from a mile off. And if you don't have the security of life insurance, it can be incredibly stressful for the whole family. This is very much an American phenomenon as well. I bet that, in most countries around the world, the leading cause of bankruptcy is job loss. Well, in the United States, the leading cause is health issues. A lot of people spend their working lives saving up and being responsible, only to have to spend everything they've got on medical bills. When they eventually die, they've got nothing to share with those who have been left behind. And if the deceased was the breadwinner, that can put the family home at risk, for example.

If only one person in a marriage works, and the other drops dead, and now there are all these debts to pay and a funeral to plan and a mortgage to maintain... you see the problem. Being able to offer a way out of that financial nightmare is a service you can feel proud of as a life insurance salesperson.

Now, I'm not sitting here saying that the industry is held up by moral do-gooders who just want to make sure everyone is okay. There is a ruthless side to the business. For life insurance policies, there is something called the "contestability period," which typically takes up the first two years of the policy.

And most companies will have a whole division of ruthless sons of bitches whose sole purpose is to find a reason not to pay out on a policy. In the movies, these sleuths usually dig up juicy, fraudulent claims: staged deaths, mariticides dressed up as accidents. In reality, it's usually something much less Hollywood.

Maybe you didn't disclose a medical condition or left things out of your medical history when signing up for a policy. Maybe you took up free solo rock climbing or motor sports and didn't let your insurer know. Maybe you weren't quite truthful about how much booze you drink and cigarettes you smoke. Or maybe, you just didn't make monthly payments like you were supposed to.

They are an insurance company; they are going to try and not pay out. If you die within that contestability period, they will order all of your medical records for review to ensure that nothing in them contradicts your application. You said on the application that you don't smoke, but here it says you told your doctor you were on half a pack a day? Well, that just voided the whole policy. It's like it never happened. You don't get your payout, and even the agent who sold you the policy loses his commission.

The vast majority of claims get paid out. But don't think that means a life insurance provider will be there when they are needed. People have to make sure they're on top of their Ps and Qs. It might seem like a trivial technicality, but that's what these people are looking for, so stay alert.

Don't get me wrong; I do love that life insurance adds value. If I had to sell something that pays really well but it was at the detriment of the people I was selling to, I wouldn't do that, so money is not the be-all, end-all.

But I have to be honest. The main reason I got into this game was the money. The industry does not lose. You can think of the insurance industry as a giant casino, with millions of people putting money in every day.

Most of those people won't ever see that money again. A minority will end up with a big payout, making the whole thing worthwhile for the customer. But the house always wins, both in Las Vegas and in the insurance industry.

A company might lose on Joe Blow's policy—he might take out life insurance, make three payments and die, and the company has to fork out $100,000. But when you put everyone in a bucket? The insurer ain't losing. There's no chance. These companies have decades—even centuries—of historical trends to back up the decisions they make regarding policies. Insurers making their money back and accruing a profit is close to a mathematical certainty; only massive anomalies or exceedingly rare events will mess up the formula.

If you look at the insurance carriers that have failed[1] over the last fifty years, you'll see one or two that went under due to unexpectedly large losses over things like asbestos claims. The reason the vast majority went under? Bad investments.

That's the thing about big insurance companies—the money they make off policies is a major cog in a wider, money-making machine. The insurer will take some

---

1   https://www.linkedin.com/pulse/20-most-notable-insurance-carrier-failures-jeff-affronti/

of the money from customers and invest it in other areas, like bonds or blue-chip stocks.

The upshot is that insurance companies contribute a significant amount to the health of the American economy. The insurance industry provides 2.9 million jobs[2] that encompass a wide variety of careers, from human resource administrators to public relations managers to financial analysts.

The insurance industry contributed $660 billion—or 2.6%—to the US gross domestic product in 2022. That's more than the agriculture and mining industries put together. In the US, life insurance alone saw total revenues of over $1 trillion[3] in 2023.

The industry is just stacked with money. It's fuck you money. And the people at the top don't want to get their hands dirty, go out into middle America, and sell all their policies. So, they incentivize a bunch of

---

2 https://www.iii.org/publications/a-firm-foundation-how-insurance-supports-the-economy/driving-economic-progress/employment

3 https://www.statista.com/statistics/214544/total-revenue-of-us-life-and-health-insurance-industry/#:~:text=In%202022%2C%20the%20life%2Fannuity,dollars%20between%202021%20and%202022.

hungry agents with fat commissions to go out and do it for them.

I joined insurance to get my hands on some of that fuck you money, and quickly found out that it's surprisingly difficult. When it comes to writing agents, the high earners represent a vanishingly small fraction of the total workforce. The vast majority of agents make very little money.

Here is the paradox of selling insurance: if it didn't pay well, most people wouldn't do this shit. And if it were easy, more people would do it, and it wouldn't pay that well.

I'll do a quick exercise to illustrate my point. I've just pulled up the progress of my agents over the last two months.

The top performer has written 104 applications worth $252,000. The second highest performer wrote 154 applications worth $229,000. The third highest performer wrote 271 applications worth $228,000. Of the agents, 195 made forty thousand or above in two months. Meanwhile, 1,702 agents made less than forty thousand, and 1,289 made under ten thousand over that period. That means that two-thirds of the agents on my books are scraping together less than five thousand a month, and just 10% of agents are making what I'd call decent money.

I hope this fires home a really important point: becoming a life insurance salesperson does not guarantee you riches. In fact, the odds dictate that the majority of people who get into the industry will never see big checks. To use the casino analogy again, most people who gamble in Vegas end up losing. I figured out a few simple ways to beat the house, and I'm sharing them with you.

One thing that's hard about selling life insurance? People don't have to have it, legally. You can operate in the world just fine without it. It's not like car insurance. Relative to life insurance, there isn't a generous upfront or per-transaction commission selling car insurance, because it is legally required. You're not going to win any awards for closing that deal.

Life insurance has some of the highest and most swiftly paid upfront commissions for agents. With life insurance, people usually have to meet a set of circumstances before they consider signing up for a policy. Around 52% of American adults[4] have life insurance. Now, you might say to me, "Wow John, that means 48% of the adult population is there for the taking!" But that's not the case. In general, single, young adults don't see the need for life insurance. They don't have a partner or kids to leave money to in the event of their death, or they don't have much money or many assets to begin with. Life-insurance coverage is lower among younger adults than in the general adult population; 40% of Gen Z and 48% of Millennials[5] had insurance in 2023. Those numbers have risen over the past few years, and there is a chance that witnessing the COVID-19 pandemic made young adults a bit more aware of their mortality.

Anyhow, despite all those nuances, the fact of the matter is that there are tens of millions of American adults without life insurance who fit the profile of a willing and eager customer: for example, Jane Smith, a parent with an income and a property.

---

4   https://www.limra.com/en/newsroom/news-releases/2023/new-study-shows-interest-in-life-insurance-at-all-time-high-in-2023/

5   https://info.limra.com/gen-zy-barometer

Now, Jane, like most people, understands the way that insurance works. She, the customer, pays me, the insurer, to take on the financial risk of an unfortunate event that may possibly occur down the line. But there are a bunch of life insurance companies, and there are a bunch of different policies. Jane might need convincing that the company I represent is reputable, or that the policy I am offering her is the right fit. Eventually, Jane decides against signing up, and we part ways.

Damn, I sure thought that Jane was gonna buy from me, I must be leaving her house defeated having lost out on that commission, right? Wrong.

As we have established, there are literally millions of Janes. I could have spent the day before calling one hundred of them, the morning calling fifty of them, and set up meetings with forty of them over the rest of the week. Success in this industry has little to do with your ability to convince Jane to buy a policy. It has a lot to do with your ability to pick up the phone and dial Janes, Jacks, and Joes until your fingers bleed.

The average American doesn't want to talk to an insurance salesperson. If you walk out front of a

Walmart and there is one table selling Girl Scout Cookies and one table selling life insurance? Everyone is leaving with a snack.

It is changing a bit these days, perhaps because of social media. Historically, the life insurance guy would be a fifty-six-year-old white dude with a briefcase. Now, being in insurance has started to be cooler. Let's be real; it's because of the money in it. Also, these days people sort of lump it in with financial services, which sounds fancier. In any case, it's cool to watch the shift.

If you Google the average life insurance salary in the US, it's $66,000. But the range is enormous. Our top guys are making over $1 million a year. You put one hundred life insurance people in a room, a couple are making real money, and a bunch are making so little it makes that average sound cool.

The funny thing is, these people are selling the same products. They have the same license and are working with the exact same tools. They are targeting the same human beings in the same country. Everything is the same.

I analyzed a whole bunch of other companies run by my buddies, and when I put all their data into my spreadsheets, it proved that all the agencies were the same. The average agent made like $350 per scheduled appointment, no matter what company, what agency, what state, or how old or young they were—the averages were the averages, regardless of the sale. It's wild to me that people want to make it more complicated than that.

The counterpoint to what I'm writing about is "work smarter, not harder." Every time I post something about the Do More concept on social media, some dipshit is in my replies writing: "Work smarter, not harder. You should get a better CRM, you should use AI, then you wouldn't have to do more."

First of all, fuck you. Second, I didn't get rich that way. I'm telling you what worked for me. And you know what? Not everyone can work smarter. I'm not the smartest guy in the room. I know for sure not everyone can manage a CRM and be successful. But you know what everyone is capable of? Making five hundred phone calls in a day. Why would I not promote a way of working that is accessible to the masses, rather than the few?

The guy who can do it smarter? High five. Good job. You are an outlier. I ain't mad at you; here is your trophy. But I'm not going to train people on your shit, because it's not applicable to the middle chunk on the bell curve where 70% of people operate as average performers. And I am one of those guys, to be clear. I am not an outlier.

Also, it's about perspective. Some lady boasted in my replies the other day that she made $300,000 only working ten hours a week due to some automation or other. I'm like, "Great, good for you. But you do know there are people out there who work 40-hour weeks and earn $900,000 a year, right? Some people are not going to settle for $300,000. Especially if thirty hours are being left on the table every week. So, if you want to kick back and not get up too much, that's fine. But don't expect everybody else to settle."

Now, both of those situations are outliers. But I swear, if you use your forty hours well—doing money making activities and following the methods I go into in this book—you will make a ton more than you do right now.

It's why I've built this whole thing. Not everyone believes in it, and that's okay. I just move on from those people. I'm just telling you guys how I did what I did, the path that I walked. If you want to try and walk it, go ahead, it's for everybody. If you don't, that's fine too.

And of course, as you go down the road, you will naturally become more efficient and do things in less time. I don't have to do what I did ten years ago to make money today. And I don't have to make the same sacrifices that I used to.

If I went to the gym at 6:00 a.m. instead of 8:00 a.m., or if I played golf at 6:00 p.m. instead of 2 p.m. on a Friday afternoon, I'd have more time to generate revenue. That's definitely a decision I would have made a decade ago. But now I'm comfortable; I don't have to make those calls any more. I just think people do that too soon.

Again, if you want to make thirty thousand dollars a year and go traveling around the country in a broken-down car, pitching tents for accommodation, more power to you. But if you complain to me that you aren't making enough, can't take care of your family, can't go on vacation, can't donate to church, and can't do all the other things you want to do, all while I'm looking at your numbers and you are simply not working... then there is a disconnect. The solution is work and sacrifice. Work and sacrifice.

CHAPTER FOUR
SEVENTEEN, OR THE NUMBER THAT CHANGED MY LIFE

"Hey kid, hurry up and get the milk in the fridge before it gets warm," yelled Tim, the clerk at the local Cumberland Farms, as he sat out front of the shop, feet propped up on a crate, chain-smoking Newports.

I must've been twelve years old at the time; Tim would chuck me a few scratch tickets and candy bars as payment for loading his shelves when new stock came in.

Tim had those glasses with the sunglasses attachment that you could flip up and down, like Dwayne Wayne wore on *A Different World*. He let me try them on once, when I went round to his place with a buddy of mine, and we smoked our first joint. Man, I wanted those glasses.

After stocking the cooler, I headed out front to offer my windshield-washing services as I did most days after school or on the weekends, when I wasn't playing wiffle ball with neighborhood kids under the nearby crabapple tree (hitting the roof of the Cumberland Farms gas station was a home run). I say *offer to wash*, but you didn't really have a say in it. I would start lashing the squeegee across your windshield no questions asked, and all you had to decide was what you were gonna pay me.

Working at the gas station took me most of that particular morning. Finally, I had done enough, and I hurried down the street with a soapy wad of dollar bills in my back pocket.

After five or so blocks, I hung a right on Broadway, and my weekend pilgrimage was complete. In front of me was the most sacred building in all of Lynn, Massachusetts: the sports card trading store.

"How ya doin', John?" Eddy, the shopkeeper, said through his big black beard. Well, Eddy was more than a shopkeeper. He was the only person I knew who was as obsessed with baseball cards as I was, and for that, he had my respect.

"I'm good, Eddy. Let's see how lucky I get today," I said, unclenching a fistful of bills onto the counter in front of him.

I took the box of baseball cards and resisted the urge to rip it open there and then. I wanted to savor the moment, plus I had a whole system.

Back home, sitting on my bed, I carefully opened the packaging. I knew the first card well. Darryl Strawberry, New York Mets, Outfield. I leafed through my booklet and inserted the card inside the sleeve that housed a handful of other cards featuring the Straw Man. I then went through my ledger to the pages marked "S" to input the latest addition.

I diligently recorded each new entry: Gary Sheffield, Milwaukee Brewers, Outfield; Barry Bonds, Pittsburgh Pirates, Left Fielder; Bob Boone, Catcher, Philadelphia Phillies; Roger Clemens, Pitcher, Boston Red Sox.

And then, there it was. A jolt of adrenaline quickened my heart as I lifted the card from the deck, inspecting it closely in all its glory. It was Bo Jackson. And not just *any* Bo Jackson. I had about twenty of his cards already, but this one was special; it had a black-and-white photo of Bo wearing shoulder pads, his hands draped over a bat resting behind his neck, nods to the two sports mastered by one of America's greatest ever athletes.

Bo Jackson, Kansas City Royals, Outfield. I logged the find in the ledger and placed the card neatly in my binder.

I was obsessed with baseball cards. Each box set had around seven hundred to eight hundred cards, and I must've had dozens of them—some bought with window-washing money, some stolen, some as gifts on Christmas and birthdays. And perhaps as much as the cards themselves, I was obsessed with tracking all the data in my ledger; I would look up the value of each card obsessively in each new *Beckett Baseball* issue.

I started tracking my own statistics playing baseball as a kid: my at-bats, my runs, my hits, my strikeouts, my stolen bases, my batting average—everything would go in my ledger.

I think I got it from my mom. I remember watching her manage our budget. We were on welfare most of my childhood, so every single cent counted. She had this whole envelope filing system and would track every dollar in and out of the house. She would literally place dollar bills in different marked envelopes, work away in her own ledger, noting down the weekly spend on groceries, our monthly energy usage, our bus and train fares. There's this saying: "Count the pennies, and the dollars will take care of themselves." It's particularly true when pretty much all you got are pennies.

Life was constantly kicking our asses, and maybe tracking and measuring stuff was my way—and my mom's way—of maintaining order and control in our small corner of the universe. As you can imagine, the first time I laid eyes on Microsoft Excel was a special day for me. I realized I'd been playing checkers, and this was chess.

When I first started selling insurance, it was second nature for me to input my progress to spreadsheets.

How many answered or unanswered calls, how many meetings, how many cancellations? Everything went into the spreadsheet. Thing is, when you start off putting data down in this way, you have no idea what you are looking for. Patterns will only present themselves once you have a large enough data set. And you can only draw accurate conclusions when you have a large enough sample size.

Think about it this way. Let's say my wife bakes some cupcakes and asks me and my son how they taste. "Amazing," we both say. "Delicious." Technically, 100% of the people who have tried the cakes liked them. But can she really trust that feedback? It's just two people, and we both have reason to not hurt her feelings by saying the cakes suck.

Now, if she takes one hundred cupcakes (a larger sample size) to a bake sale and word gets out about how delicious—or disastrous—the cakes are, she can take the number of cakes remaining at the end of the day as a better indication of their quality.

I'm sure I'm not the first insurance salesperson to start manually tracking their progress in a spreadsheet. But I bet not many stuck with it as long as I did. What's the point of tracking everything, right? You either book the meeting, or you don't. You either make the sale, or you don't.

If it wasn't for my obsession with measurement, I probably would've stopped tracking everything too. But I had a sneaking suspicion that the pattern would start to show itself. And sure enough, it did.

Being a salesperson can be a thankless task. You're endlessly dialing, people rarely pick up, and when they do, they don't want to hear from you. It feels like the juice isn't worth the squeeze most of the time.

But when I started tracking my calls, I saw that wasn't the case. In January 2013, my first year in insurance, I made 252 calls that month, 28 contacts, and 23 appointments. I was sitting there thinking I was getting beat up, that nothing was going my way. But since I'd tracked my stats, I could see that 82% of the people I'd spoken to had booked an appointment.

I get a little pep in my step. This ain't so bad. Fast-forward to the end of the year. I'd made just under sixty thousand dollars—not amazing, but it was okay—

and honestly, I was fired up because I could commit full-time to insurance.

I inputted a simple formula to my spreadsheet: my total deposits divided by the number of dials I'd placed.

$58,983.10 / 3,558 = $16.58

This changed my view on insurance, and it changed my life. I saw that every single time I picked up the phone, no matter what the outcome, I made seventeen dollars. If you didn't pick up, seventeen bucks. If you told me to fuck off, seventeen bucks. If you strung me along and then didn't book an appointment, seventeen bucks. I checked my dials versus contacts and saw that people would only pick up 10% of the time. This meant that 90% of phone calls were spent doing nothing but listening to a dial tone. But it didn't matter. Seventeen bucks.

I went into 2014 with a new attitude. Before, I looked at my phone with dread each morning, wondering what level of rejection and bullshit lay on the other end of the line. Now, I looked at it as a money printing machine.

The formula had also given me an enormous reality check. In 2013, I made an average of 296 calls a month. Let's say each one lasts a minute on average, since most people don't pick up. That's five hours a month on the phone.

To quote Matthew McConaughey's character in *The Wolf of Wall Street*: "You gotta pump those numbers up. Those are rookie numbers."

I said to myself: *John, you idiot. You make seventeen dollars every time you call. Why are you only spending five hours a month working the phone?* I had been hunting for greatness in all the wrong places. The answer had been in front of me the whole time, hidden within my spreadsheets. Thank God I'd stuck with it until the sample size had grown large enough for that magic number to reveal itself to me.

It wasn't about what suit I wore, what car I drove, what jokes I made to leads. It was a simple numbers game.

I call inputting that formula my "Moneyball moment." *Moneyball* is a 2011 baseball film—based on a book of the same name—that documents the Oakland Athletics

2002 season. In the film, the team's general manager, Billy Beane, is struggling to remain competitive with limited resources. That year, Oakland had a payroll of $40 million; meanwhile, financial powerhouses like the Boston Red Sox and the New York Yankees are working with budgets in excess of $100 million. Baseball and a shoe-string budget? You can see why this story might have spoken to me.

The league is so unfair that it's basically rigged, and Beane knows he has to think outside of the box if he wants any chance at success.

There is a scene in the movie where Beane is losing patience in a meeting with his scouts. It's a room full of elderly veterans of the scouting game, and Brad Pitt sticks out like a sore thumb.

They're discussing some recruitment targets.

"I like Geronimo; he's an athlete. Clean-cut, good face."

"He passes the eye candy test. He's got the looks; he's ready to play the part."

Later in the movie, there's a second scout meeting, and this time, Beane brings in a new hire: Peter Brand, played by Jonah Hill. Brand is obsessed with statistics and convinced that the traditional way of putting a team together is wrong. He's collected enough data that the patterns have started to emerge in front of him.

He's noticed that the old scouts are overlooking a bunch of cheap players for bad reasons ("He's got an ugly girlfriend; ugly girlfriend means no confidence"), whereas in Brand's system, *all* that matters is if they can execute the task at hand reliably. It doesn't matter if they are too old, too slow, too fat, or too volatile. If they get on base enough, there is room for them in the roster.

"This is the new direction of the Oakland A's," Beane says. "We are card counters at the blackjack table, and we are going to turn the odds on the casino."

This low-cost, low-profile team ultimately goes on a twenty-game unbeaten run, and Beane and Brand's empirical, analytical approach is adopted by teams across the league.

I imagined life insurance recruiters talked about salespeople the same way the old-school talent scouts do in the movie.

"He's got some killer one-liners."

"He pulls up to meetings in a Mercedes, very impressive."

"He's got more confidence than Sinatra at a karaoke party."

Cool. How many calls did he make last month? 175? I'm sorry; he's not getting the job.

The realization that my performance would correlate directly with my call volume was incredibly freeing. This was quantifiable and within my control. It wasn't some intangible thing like confidence, humor, compassion, the ability to put a client "at ease," or any other so-called "secret to sales success." It was all a simple math problem.

What I loved most about it was that if I looked at *activity* versus *deposits* on my spreadsheet, it factored in all the bullshit everyone hated: cancels, no-shows, chargebacks, getting kicked out of houses. It was all factored in, and I *still* got seventeen dollars a call. That was the most freeing part to me. A weight had been lifted.

You want to make $100,000 next year? Great, go make six thousand calls. You want to make $170,000? Mash those buttons ten thousand times.

This insight would never have occurred to me if I hadn't been grinding and learning on the job. I had to pump out a year of well-intentioned but inefficient work before I had the tools and knowledge to start killing the game. I had to Do More Now and Get Better Later.

After I explain all this to salespeople, I get a frequent reply.

"That's great and all John, but I really don't know my way around Excel, and formulas look like Greek to me."

First off, I don't believe you. For the *vast* majority of people, there is no such thing as naturally being bad at math. You just haven't put the time in to learn. Not to mention, the above stuff is like fourth grade math, not advanced calculus.

Second, don't worry about it. I have done the work for you. I have designed an activity tracker that tracks all your data: your dials, your contacts, your appointments, everything. All you have to do is take thirty seconds a day to input your information, and you will have raised your chances of success exponentially.

My whole team uses this system, and we are constantly improving and updating our automated services so the same principles of measurement and data analysis can improve every aspect of a firm's operation.

But before you download my tracker, there is a really easy exercise iPhone users can perform to see if they are on track in terms of output and productivity. After a call day, I want you to take out your phone, open your call history, and scroll down to the bottom. The phone stores your last one hundred calls. Now read out the date and time of the oldest call. If it was today, good job, you're on track. If it was yesterday, or three days ago, I'm sorry, you've got work to do. (Sidenote: iPhone has updated since I came up with this and now stores one thousand calls. But you get the point!)

I do this exercise with new recruits all the time. They'll look through their phones and sometimes the one hundredth call will be nine days or more ago. In this industry, on a dial day, it should be no more than a few hours ago.

Above all else, it's imperative that you put the reps in. A helpful way of getting this across is the *10,000-hours rule*, popularized by the Canadian journalist and author Malcolm Gladwell. In his book *Outliers: The Story of Success*, Gladwell often comes back to the general rule of thumb that it takes 10,000 hours to master something.

For example, the Beatles amassed 10,000 hours of playing time in just four years as they took over the music world. And Bill Gates spent more than 10,000 hours in the computer room at high school to master programming.

I think that a lot of people misinterpret the point that Gladwell is making in this book. He is not saying that if you spend 10,000 hours playing basketball, you can expect to play in the NBA. Of course, talent matters, and two people who put the same amount of time and effort into something can expect different results at the end of the day. If a young Usain Bolt and I spend 10,000 hours working on our sprints, we are both going to improve our times drastically, but only one of us is going to set world records at the Olympics.

What I think is important about the 10,000-hours rule is that it is a powerful metaphor for the surprising amount of effort it takes to succeed at something. There is simply no way around it. The amount of commitment you need in order to master something is no joke.

The same goes for my industry. If you want results, that one hundredth call in your phone better not be from yesterday; it has to be from today. If you want to make a six-figure income, you are going to need to pump up the volume. You need to put the hours and the calls in, and a great way to make sure you don't fall behind is to ensure that you meticulously track everything.

Armed with data, you can analyze your strengths and weaknesses, identifying areas for improvement like a coach dissecting game film. You can set specific, measurable goals and track your progress religiously, treating each milestone as a victory.

The big thing that comes out of tracking and measuring is seeing how performance averages out over time. I remember early on in my career, there was a guy named Ray who worked on the sales team.

Ray was a super charismatic guy—good-looking, well turned out—he had the gift of the gab. You know that phrase "guys want to be him, girls want to be with him"? Yeah, that was Ray.

It seemed that leads just couldn't wait to part with their money when Ray walked in the room. And it showed in his numbers. Or did it really?

You see, when Ray turned it on, he was hard to beat. Results came through for sales one February and sure enough, Ray was on top of the leaderboard. He'd made himself thirty thousand dollars that month, nothing to sneeze at. Meanwhile, I'd put in the third best performance that month.

July rolled around, and once again, Ray came out on top; this time, I was in second.

"Don't sweat it, Wetmore, your time will come, I'm sure," Ray said, flashing an arrogant smile. I'm not going to lie, it stung. But I didn't have to worry. You see, come the end of the year, I was the top salesman by a country mile. I earned $460,000, and Ray came in a distant second with $250,000.

I had top sales for maybe four weeks out of fifty-two. But I was consistently second, or third, or fourth, and always in the top ten. Overall, my average blew everyone else out of the water. And I maintained steady and consistent targets thanks to obsessively tracking every metric and sticking to predetermined targets.

Meanwhile, Ray ended up with $200,000 less than me by the end of the year. You see, he would absolutely smash it out the park one month, and then totally coast the next few months, resting on his laurels. He'd win bragging rights two or three times a year, but in reality, these were hollow victories. Ray was not even close to being the top earner, because he never held himself accountable.

Don't be Ray. Improve on your personal best whenever you can and track your progress. Slowly but surely, the tide will begin to turn. With each passing month, your numbers will climb higher.

Before long, the results will speak for themselves. Tracking progress isn't just a tool—it's a mindset. It's about holding yourself accountable, going beyond your limits, and refusing to settle for anything less than greatness. Whether you're chasing sales targets or personal goals, the spreadsheet serves as a compass, guiding you towards victory one data point at a time.

The true turning point will come when you embrace the concept of continuous improvement—the idea that greatness isn't achieved overnight, but through relentless effort and self-reflection. Like an athlete honing their craft in the offseason, commit yourself to constant growth, always striving to outperform your previous best.

To help you get there, let's revisit that handy acronym I spelled out in the introduction to this book:

DISCIPLINE
OWNERSHIP

MISTAKES
OBSESSION
RESILIENCE
EXPECTATIONS

CHAPTER FIVE
DISCIPLINE

I don't know if they still do, but Wendy's used to have these kid's nights, where junior meals were $1.99, and they gave out balloon animals.

Kids could get these spray-on tattoos—on their arms, legs, torsos. We had a loosely enforced "not the face" rule, but even so, my wife inevitably had a tricky clean-up job on her hands before school the next day.

Maddox would run around with a balloon sword, doing his best pirate impression, and his older siblings would fall over themselves laughing. Even I had to admit, it was pretty funny.

I had my first kid when I was seventeen and my second at twenty. As my tribe grew over the years,

I learned the value of picking a place with simple food and small games to keep everyone occupied and having fun. Herding cats is a lot easier when they're all headed towards the same treat or trinket.

Wendy's was a tradition I looked forward to each Wednesday with Maddox (my son with Steph), Brayden, and Gabby (two of four kids from my previous marriage). My eldest, Shailey, was off to college at this point; meanwhile, TJ was of driving age, so he wasn't around a ton.

It was a time to bond with my children and learn about their challenges and victories over the past week in the classroom or on the sports field. After Wendy's, we'd usually go on to do some activity like karate at the county facility, or gymnastics, or play for hours at the playground, the kids making each other dizzy on the merry-go-round and then running and catching each other, laughing hysterically when they inevitably face-planted in the mulch.

But something was nagging at me at this particular dinner. Wednesdays just weren't working out. I was making calls on a Monday and heading out to appointments on a Tuesday. I'd make calls on a

Wednesday, unable to hit the road as it was Wendy's night. That left Thursday for a second day of appointments; then, every other Friday I was picking the kids up from school. I needed to figure out a way to up my appointment count—and fast.

I had a chat with my good friend and professional mentor Mike Killimett about the situation, and he told me I would never really catch any momentum working one day on, one day off.

Meanwhile, I noticed a fellow agent, Marc Meade, was crushing it, and I wanted to know how. What was his secret? Was he flashing a smile before delivering a killer line that wrapped up the sale then and there? Did he enter the room wearing the perfect suit—not so flashy to be intimidating, but just stylish enough to show he meant business? If I could have figured out the magic pill, it would have made the whole thing a lot easier.

I approached Marc once at an event. He had just finished a thirty-minute speech outlining how he'd reached over $600,000 the previous year. A lot of his backstory resonated with me. He'd come from mortgages and dealt with the same issues I had when the crash came. He'd started out in insurance $250,000 in debt, which he was able to pay off in just twelve months. He had a no-nonsense, *get shit done* attitude, a mantra I continue to live by and that I have plastered all over my office (as well as on hoodies, hats, and other merchandise on my site:

The talk was centered around what he saw as the most important aspects of the whole insurance game: leads and appointments. Everything else was just noise to Marc.

When he was done speaking, I chased him down, wanting to get more from him, trying to figure out how I could go from mediocre to great. I kept asking how he did it, and he said, "Bro, did you just miss my entire talk?"

I was sure there had to be more specifics. Maybe he had better quality leads, or perhaps there was a particular time I should have been dialing? What was his script, his lead vendor; what products did he sell?

He ignored my questions and simply asked how many appointments I was running. I knew my spreadsheet inside-out and told him I averaged forty-two appointments a month.

Now, anyone that knows Marc will tell you that he has a very distinctive laugh that will escape him spontaneously during moments of disbelief.

Sure enough, when I said the number forty-two, I got a serious helping of the Marc-Meade-laugh.

"How do you expect my results with your work ethic?" Marc asked.

"That's a really good question, bro," I replied casually, but his comment hit me like a line drive.

After leaving the event and spending a day or so thinking over his questions, I texted Marc and asked: "So, how many appointments do you run?"

His very simple reply was one I'll never forget in my life: "90+++"

You see, I've always worked hard. Having kids this young kind of forces that on you. The more mouths there are to feed, the more hours there are to work. I put in seventy-hour weeks straight out of high school.

But the numbers didn't lie. Marc was putting in more reps than I was, even with kids of his own to worry about. I needed to figure out a way to work harder.

That night after dinner at Wendy's, I went home to Steph, and we mapped out my schedule. It became immediately obvious that Wednesday was a dead zone, a black hole that sucked up any opportunity for increased productivity in my week.

I'd spent so much time trying to figure out what the "magic pill" was that I'd lost sight of a simple truth that I'd learned years ago working that warehouse job.

The bosses in the warehouse would crack the whip constantly, judging your efficiency by how quickly you could drive the pallet jacks up and down the aisle, loading and unloading trucks for deliveries.

I always set my jack to slow, or what we all called "turtle mode," which pissed off my supervisors to no end. I joke about turtle mode to this day; I may look like I'm moving slowly, but I'm getting more shit done than most.

"Everyone else is flying around; it's like the Daytona 500 in here, and you can't even get out of first gear, John?" my supervisor once said.

I patiently asked him to check my record. You see, I knew I was completing more orders faster than anyone else in the warehouse because I'd taken the time to plan it all out. I didn't just mindlessly bring all the pallets over to the truck and dump them there.

I paid attention to the order in which different items needed to be loaded and unloaded, which hugely increased the efficiency of the system. By spending a small amount of time plotting a strategy and being methodical in my approach, I was able to outcompete everyone else in the warehouse, no matter how fast they were zooming about the place.

As soon as the supervisors saw that I was working with a delivery score of 120%—a full fifth above the target most would struggle to meet—they let me go about my business uninterrupted.

"It's just like the warehouse," I said to Steph. "I can make as many calls as I want, but what's the point of all that groundwork if I haven't figured out the most efficient way to execute?"

Marc was running 90+ appointments a month, and I was sitting at forty-two, despite putting similar hours in each day—in my head anyways.

I wasn't going to ditch dinner with the kids, that was nonnegotiable. I could give my kids all the money in the world, but if I didn't give them my time as well, it would all be meaningless to them.

Steph and I figured out that if I moved dinner with the kids from Wednesday to Thursday, it opened up the number of appointments I could make on Monday, and I could commit Tuesday and Wednesday to working in the field. Throw in every other Friday when I didn't have the kids, plus one Saturday a month for good measure, and I could blow my previous numbers out of the water.

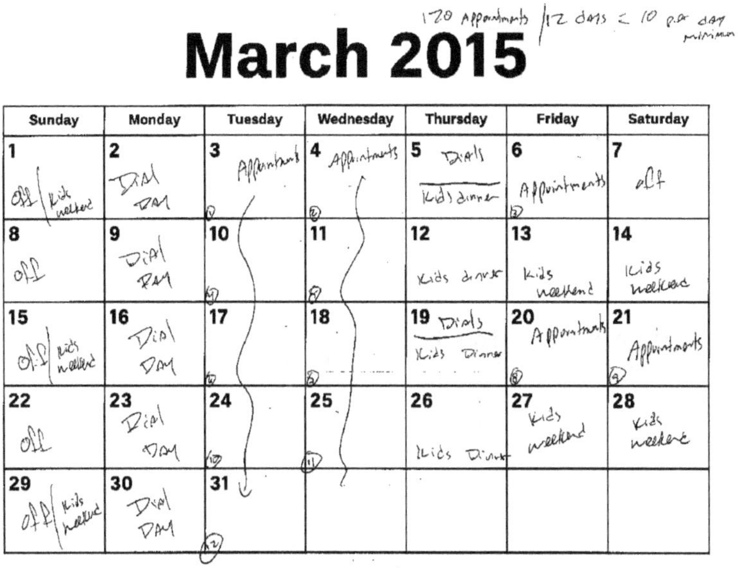

March 2015

Handwritten annotation at top: 120 Appointments / 12 days = 10 per day minimum

Sunday	Monday	Tuesday	Wednesday	Thursday	Friday	Saturday
1 off / kids weekend	**2** Dial Day	**3** Appointments	**4** Appointments	**5** Dials / Kids dinner	**6** Appointments	**7** off
8 off	**9** Dial Day	**10**	**11**	**12** Kids dinner	**13** Kids weekend	**14** Kids weekend
15 off / kids weekend	**16** Dial Day	**17**	**18**	**19** Dials / Kids Dinner	**20** Appointments	**21** Appointments
22 off	**23** Dial Day	**24**	**25**	**26** Kids Dinner	**27** Kids weekend	**28** Kids weekend
29 off / kids weekend	**30** Dial Day	**31**				

The difference was drastic. With the above schedule, I had 12 field days a month, averaging 10 appointments a day, meaning if I stayed on track, it would be 120 per month, or 1,500 appointments a year—on only 11 days a month selling. Even with a crappy closing rate of 25%, at a thousand bucks a pop I'd make more money than I'd ever seen. Suddenly, the life that lay ahead of me and my family took on a different appearance. And I liked the look of it.

In that life, I could send my kids to private school. In that life, I'd never think about making rent again. I could put a few hundred dollars in the donation bin at church, instead of ten. I could take my family on vacation. I could sit in the front of the plane. And maybe above all else, in that life, I would be mentally present during the time I spent with my wife and kids—not preoccupied with the work I hadn't done, not stressing about the problems I could only solve with income I didn't have.

Then came the tricky question...would my ex-wife go for it? We'd kept a good relationship but navigating divorce is tough at times, and she had her own commitments to meet.

It's a funny thing making a call like that. So much was riding on a silly thing like moving dinner from Wednesday to Thursday. Literally, hundreds of thousands of dollars. If you factor in the opportunity costs, my Wednesdays at Wendy's could've become some of the most expensive meals in America.

"I don't give a crap what day you have dinner with them," my ex-wife said over the phone as I breathed a sigh of relief. "They just want to see you."

With her sign-off, I had my schedule and stuck it to the fridge. I was going to be MIA from my marriage on

Tuesday and Wednesday, out on the road, sometimes ending the day three hours from home.

No more sleeping in. When you look at disciplined people, getting up early is one hell of a commonality.

I had figured out the numbers game; now it was about having the discipline to execute. I wanted to show others that I could make this change. I wanted to show them that I could become a leader.

> *Discipline is the ability to take action when there's no motivation or proof (i.e., no results). And consistency is the ability to do those things for an extended amount of time.*
>
> — Jef Quin

Maddox had hot tears streaming down his face.

"I don't want to go to football practice," he cried. He'd started out complaining about not feeling that well, but we had now morphed into a full-on meltdown.

"You've gotta go, bud," I said to him. "You're part of a team, and that means showing up even when you don't want to."

We'd just come back from a vacation in Florida where he'd experienced neighborhood living for the first time. Instead of having to rely on car rides to play dates, he had been zooming around on his bike all day visiting various friends who'd joined us in Seaside, Florida for the week.

After experiencing that kind of independence and freedom for the first time, getting back to the grind of his regular schedule was a shock to his system, especially after a long flight and little sleep.

"Can I let you in on a secret, buddy?" I said. "Half the time I go to the gym or work, I don't want to do it. But I think about what would happen to me—and all of us—if I stopped taking care of myself or my family. And that's what motivates me. If you stop showing up to practice, if you didn't have football in your life, how would that make you feel?"

Maddox saw his friends and teammates jump out of their parents' cars and walk together through the parking lot. He began to wipe the tears from his face.

"Now, you can tell the coach you're not feeling so good today, and you might want to sit this one out on the sidelines," I said. "But you've got to show up."

He had a blast that day. The coach said he made some amazing plays. He was totally in his element back among his teammates doing what he loved.

We laughed about it later, when he called me "Do More Dad." He likes to give me crap.

I am by no means the perfect parent, and at times, I might go hard on my kids. But I think it's so important to instill in them that, when things get tough and you feel like giving up, you have to push on through in order to get the results you want in the long run. Short-term pain for long-term gain.

It took me so much effort to get in good shape, and it's always funny to me when people ask how I did it. Everyone knows what the answer is here, but they're still hoping someone will give them the "magic pill" from the infomercial. Unfortunately, it's a far more boring answer: I lift something heavy, or I sweat. Every day.

I used to go to the gym two or three times a week and eat like crap. It wasn't until I made a commitment to get some work in—any work—on a daily basis that the noticeable results started coming through. Before that, I was just maintaining.

All of us have the tools and the experience to keep up a schedule for hard work.

The patterns we follow every day are a type of discipline. We wake up, we go to our jobs, we prepare meals, we shower, and we watch our favorite TV shows. Some of these things are requirements, some we do as second nature, and some give us comfort. But it's all a pattern. We are pattern-seeking animals.

Sometimes, I hear people talk about wishing they had a "business mindset," which would give them more discipline and stick-to-itiveness. This frustrates the hell out of me. If anything, the ability to embrace the grind of a tough, demanding schedule is an "employee mindset."

I would observe agents at work who had been crazy successful, trying to find what they had in common. The answer, confusingly, was not much. They had different scripts, different styles, different deliveries. Some were naturally funny people who would deliver jokes to break the ice. Some were more sensible: a safe pair of hands.

The common thread? They had figured out that showing up consistently was the key to it all.

When I realized that boosting my sales numbers had little to do with how convincing my pitch was or what car I pulled up in, and more to do with discipline and maintaining a consistent schedule, it was freeing.

It meant I could be confident in my skin; I didn't have to pretend to be someone I wasn't. I just had to apply the skills I had, which are skills most of us are capable of adopting and adapting.

All of us are disciplined, but a lot of us are disciplined about the wrong stuff. The decision to acknowledge my capacity for discipline—and then point that discipline in the right direction—is what changed the trajectory of my life and gave me a competitive advantage in the industry.

I stopped trying to be the best sales guy; I stopped trying to be the best recruiter. I stopped trying so hard to be the perfect someone else. I could be myself at appointments—all I needed to do was figure out how to get myself to *more* of them.

This meant being meticulous about my time and preparing everything well in advance. Imagine a Patriots coach showing up to practice and saying, "Okay, boys, what're we doing today?" It probably wouldn't go down well.

The coach needs to scout the opposition, identify strategies and targets, and come up with a plan of action to ensure every goal is met on time.

To maximize the number of appointments I could achieve in a month, I had to map everything out and prepare ahead of time.

This meant meals prepped, outfits picked out, and the car packed up, all on the evening before hitting the road. I couldn't afford the mental energy and stress of running around the house looking for stuff when it was go-time.

Information on all of my leads was printed out and ready to be quickly digested before I hit each location. I'd often arrive at an appointment early, pull over near the house, and hit the phones to set up meetings for the following day. Oftentimes, I needed to overbook, knowing that people were bound to cancel or no-show me.

I started treating it like a sport or a military operation. If I planned ahead enough, I'd be in a flow state when it was time to execute. Preparation goes hand in hand with discipline.

Beforehand, I'd been consistently inconsistent. I'd crush it one week and then slack off the next three, sleeping in late, not hitting the phones as hard as usual. So, I'd end up with a mediocre month.

In 2015, my breakout year, I was only the top sales guy for a handful of weeks out of the year. At the end of the year, I issued $460,000 of life insurance premium—around 400 policies—on my own pen. And the number two guy ended up on $250,000. There were a lot of people who were ahead of me week in and week out. But there were very few people who were consistently in the top two.

I became known as the most consistent person in the office. I did this for two-and-a-half years, grinding day in and day out. I sold $1.2 million of life insurance over that period. This got the attention of the higher-ups. Most people are undisciplined; it's the norm. The managers at the company were always on the lookout for people who were different, and being disciplined made me stand out like crazy.

Within two years of sticking that schedule on my fridge, I was out of the field and teaching my methods. I started analyzing other agents' progress within our company, adapting my activity tracker so it could be used for others. I would show people what they earned per booked appointment. I let them know what their averages were—and what they could be if they upped their game. Every quarter, I'd compare the previous quarter and share success stories, highlighting the power of the simple formulas I was working with. This started attracting a ton of agents. People wanted to find out who this Wetmore guy was that could make money so simply; it was almost like he was "tricking you into getting rich."

We went from eight agents in March 2015 to 104 selling agents by the end of 2017, and that earned me $1.8 million in commissions that year—up from $100,000 in 2014.

"I'm not interested in life insurance, Mr. Wetmore, and frankly, I don't appreciate your sarcastic tone." A door slammed in my face as I was kicked out onto the street from an appointment gone wrong.

Increasing the number of calls and appointments I made only got me so far. Maintaining or improving the number of leads I converted into sales was the end goal. And I had to ensure that I responded to the feedback I received from potential customers.

When you're speaking with so many people each day, it's easy to lose track of individual interactions. If you're not careful, every call or meeting can blend into a giant mess in your mind, and you'll lose the ability to nail down valuable lessons from the ones that went well, or the ones where you bombed.

I started jotting down notes in the giant spreadsheet that contained all of my appointments. Every sale, every mess-up, every lead that remained warm—all would be scrutinized in a shorthand that served as a reminder to up my game.

I started being super transparent about mistakes that I was making, missing sales, and getting feedback that I didn't like.

Sometimes, people would just quit on me or get frustrated with me. Sometimes, I'd get kicked out of houses for being too rude or sarcastic. At that moment, it's easy to go, "What was that guy's problem?" But I knew that the problem laid with me—I'd read the room wrong, and my tone was off. If I didn't own my own shortcomings, I wasn't going to improve.

Mike has another saying: "Do you want to be right, or do you want to be rich?"

Kind of a blunt take on the "customer is always right" cliché, and I appreciated his boldness.

I generally can't stand reading, as I read slowly and wander off in my mind, forgetting what I'd just read.

At this stage, I hadn't read anything since high school. Wanting to improve, I started flicking through some books on mindset. This helped me adjust my attitude and work on my many mistakes.

Failure can make you feel worthless or stupid. It can drain you of motivation to try again, because what's the point, right? You're just going to mess it up once more. But failure is an opportunity to react to valuable feedback, increasing your chances of nailing it the next time.

Take Tom Brady, for instance. Patriots coach Bill Belichick surprised a lot of people when he said Brady was "not a great natural athlete." I guess you only have to look at Brady's combine photo to see there was some truth to that—in a league full of athletic freaks, Brady started out looking like a normal dude.

But he put more hours in than anyone working on his throwing mechanics, analyzing every error in his search for minuscule improvements, which added up over time. And he became the greatest quarterback in history along the way.

Perhaps worse than a fear of failure is a denial of failure. If you can't own your own mistakes, if your first and second instinct is to pin your screw-up on someone else, there's zero room for growth.

I had a habit of wanting to prove I was right in certain situations. But that phrase stuck with me: "Do you want to be right, or do you want to be rich?"

Parking my ego at the door, I entered a period of...let's call it "self-reflection." How did others perceive me in those moments of conflict? I had a strong suspicion that my directness might have had something to do with it, as well as a bit of obliviousness when it came to reading others.

I've never beaten around the bush. If I believe something, I'll tell you straight. And if you're feeling uncomfortable, there's a good chance I might miss that, too, which can make the whole situation a bit of a minefield from the get-go.

The thing is, I was super ignorant. I thought everyone was like me—that we all thought the same. I didn't get that my directness could be intimidating or even abrasive to some, and I definitely didn't understand why people reacted so differently.

However, my failures and mistakes in appointments forced me to take stock and do some serious learning. I began focusing on body language and studying up on communication and personality types.

Not to try and change who I was or enter the room as a different person—it just allowed me to understand which aspects of myself I needed to turn up or tone down, in response to the feedback I was getting from others.

I learned that if someone gets upset or frustrated, I need to get out of "sales mode" immediately and just talk to them as a human being. That wall is not going to come down if someone is in distress and you're just pitching at them like a sales robot.

It's funny; getting good at this at work really helped me elsewhere in life. I became a better listener, more empathetic, more capable of seeing things from the viewpoint of friends and family.

As my schedule grew and sales began to improve, I was hooked. The constant reps meant I was making more money, and I was also improving on myself. I sought more and more advice from mentors and anyone around me who I felt had something to offer.

If a speaker asked during a training session, "Do you have any questions?" I'd be like, "Yeah, I've got nine." I would wear people out quizzing them.

My obsession with improvement grew as I learned and achieved more and more.

I know what you're thinking. *Sounds great, John, but my life is so busy already; how could I possibly cram any more into my schedule? All the discipline in the world won't create more hours in the day.*

I get it, I really do. I had the same reaction when I realized that some guys had literally double the appointments I did, meanwhile, I felt I was running on fumes and had nothing more to give. I figured these guys must have been bachelors; they couldn't possibly have had my level of out-of-the-office responsibilities. But then I'd find out they had families, pets, properties, elderly parents, and any number of things that make all of our lives that bit more complicated and stressful.

One of the differences between me and those guys? They were asking for help. From colleagues, mentors, loved ones, and anyone who was willing and able to support them.

When I looked for support from professional mentors, I got better. When I asked my ex to switch up dinner night, my schedule blew wide open. And when I leveled with Steph and told her that, in order to provide the life we wanted, I would have to lean on her, she stepped up and gave me all the support in the world.

I was thirty-seven years old when we had that talk. Perhaps that's late in the day to turn your life upside-down, but I think she saw the potential in this new way of life the same way I did. I was going to be the first in the office making calls at 7:30 a.m. I was going to be up at 5:00 a.m. and on the road all of Tuesday and Wednesday. We weren't going to see each other, basically. And she needed to take on groceries, school runs, all of it, while working a full-time job of her own. Talk about discipline.

When my appointments doubled, then tripled, I just couldn't contribute to the running of the household anymore, and she took all that stress off my shoulders. We suffered—of course we did. During the work week, it was like we barely saw each other. But she never once gave me any shit for being gone, because we were both pulling in the same direction with the same goal in sight, and that meant resentment didn't build.

Seeking help from my many mentors has had a huge impact on my life. And I do mean many. I figure why have one mentor when you can take the good (and ignore the bad) from several people with proven track records?

In the past, I may have been too stubborn or proud to approach anyone with my problems. I'd sit there grappling with an issue, tying myself up in knots or ending up back where I started in search of solutions.

Learning to ask for support was transformative. First, being able to pick up the phone and say "Listen, I need your help" is immediately relieving. Just saying the words out loud lessens the burden.

Then, once you've done it enough times, you start to think like your mentor, and often that's enough. These days, when I'm confronted with an issue, oftentimes I am able to simply ask myself "What would Mike do?" and a path forward will open up to me.

Otherwise, the answer is to give it forty-eight hours. I was notorious for being impatient with my problems—the type to say "let's grab the bull by the horns and get it done." Whereas in reality, letting things play out for a bit is often the best strategy. It gives you time to focus on the many other balls you've got in the air. It's chess, not checkers; sometimes, a good move can turn into a killer blow if you wait one or two more turns before you strike.

CHAPTER SIX
OWNERSHIP

"**H**ey honey, the insurance guy is here," the man said, looking through me, not at me, before turning on his heels and heading indoors.

Great. I knew how this was gonna go.

"Look, buddy, can you just tell me what the prices are? Let's make this quick," he said flippantly, fixing himself a drink on his kitchen island.

"I'm good, thanks, how are you?" I said like a wise-ass, knowing the words were wrong as soon as they came out; but it was too late to stuff them back in my fat mouth.

He looked up at me quickly, a flicker of surprise and confusion breaking beyond the front of alpha energy he'd obviously spent years trying to perfect.

"What was that?" he said.

"I mean, I just walked into your house, dude," I continued, against my better judgment. "Not even a 'hello.' You're asking for numbers. I don't even know you yet."

"Well, you might not get to know me if you keep up like that," he replied, his face reddening with each second.

"Bro, you filled out the form," I went on, knowing now the sale was a lost cause, so screw it. "You knew I was coming to your house; now you're acting like you don't want me here? If it's an inconvenience, why did you request it?"

"Well, you can find your ass out the door then," he barked, with a face that said: *I am* this *close to kicking your ass*. He was a big boy, too, in case you were wondering.

I crumpled up the lead in my hand and tossed it behind me as I walked down the driveway toward my car, as I had done before more times than I care to admit. If you have developed a signature *fuck you* move in the sales industry, it's probably a good sign that you need to change.

By nature, I don't like people. I mean, I like certain people, but I'm not seeking out crowds or new people to meet. And unfortunately, my lack of patience with people often showed.

I want to say that was the fastest and worst sales appointment I'd had that particular month, but that would be lying.

That (dis)honor went to an elderly lady who wouldn't let me in her house. I was standing in the doorway, the kitchen was right there, but she didn't want to let me in the house.

"I don't know you, can—" she replied.

"Here, take out my ID," I said, pushing my wallet into her hand. "Now if I take anything, you've got a name to give the cops."

She looked at me, stunned.

"Okay, okay, take back your wallet," she said, visibly uncomfortable now.

"Great, so we're good?" I went on, before muttering under my breath, "Thing is, if I really wanted to rip you off, I would have made a fake ID."

I probably crumpled up and tossed the lead from that appointment, too, which couldn't have lasted more than a couple of minutes.

It certainly took her longer than that to locate my name and details, call corporate, and let them know how she thought the meeting went—in fairly colorful language.

It was Mike who got in touch with me about the complaint, and he used a phrase that has stuck with me to this day.

"Whitmore," he said, intentionally screwing up my name as had become tradition. "We need to talk about your bedside manner."

"Oh yeah, is it bad?" I asked.

"It's worse than that. You don't have one," said Mike.

>
> Culture shock (noun): *feelings of uncertainty, confusion, or anxiety that people may experience when moving to a new country or experiencing a new culture or surroundings*[6].

I'd been aware that I came off a bit rough around the edges ever since I started mixing in more middle-class or well-to-do communities in the South. Southern hospitality is real, and it came as a big shock to the system.

You don't see strangers exchanging pleasantries in the projects of Boston. If someone you don't know makes eye contact and strikes up a conversation, it's usually a really bad sign.

In the South, if you don't look people in the eye, it's seen as rude. I needed to relearn social cues and body language that had been ingrained in me for years, some of which was linked to survival.

---

6   https://www.investopedia.com/terms/c/culture-shock.asp

I remember playing this game as a kid where me and my buddies would race down the stairs from the top floor of the apartment to the lobby elevators. What made it extra challenging was having to hurdle over the occasional junky passed out in the stairwell.

From my own apartment block to the street to the grocery store, most of my time was spent dodging interactions with people. Keeping a low profile and keeping to myself was what kept me safe. When it came to basic etiquette, I was a rookie in the South.

Bedside manner (phrase): a doctor's approach or attitude to a patient

In truth, I'd never even heard the term *bedside manner*. My upbringing had left me with an instinct to approach people with suspicion, not sympathy. But I also started to get this nagging feeling that there was more to it than that—beyond how I grew up. I started to feel like I was wired differently.

For as long as I can remember, I've had a true fear of dogs. The bigger they are, the worse it is. A German shepherd, or a Doberman, something that's above my knees? No thank you. Sometimes, I'd be at a sales meeting in the kitchen with a big ole dog milling around my legs, and I would feel the sweat pricking through my pores while trying to deliver my pitch.

I've never actually been bitten. I think they freak me out because I can't read their behavior well. Most people might be able to tell when a dog is docile, friendly, or expressing aggression. I just can't make it out; all I see is sharp teeth. Dogs can smell the fear on me and that makes them agitated, even if they weren't beforehand.

It feels the same way with people sometimes. I'm not empathetic by default. I've always found it difficult to read subtle cues. If you're not direct, if you hint at something, it's going right over my head.

I joke that my wife speaks in code sometimes. It took me far too long to figure out that "Did you leave your hoodie in the car?" meant "I've left some crap in the car that I want you to get for me."

When she says, "I've taken your contacts and lotions off the bathroom counter and put them in the top drawer," that, in fact, means: "The cleaner is coming today, and you left your mess out again."

These sound like silly examples, but they used to drive me crazy. I'm not Sherlock Holmes. I don't have access to the Enigma Machine. Why choose to be so indirect? Why waste time trying to make it seem like you're not asking me to do something when that's the end goal?

For the longest time, I thought that everyone was like me. That we were all stumbling through life frustrated and constantly misunderstood. I thought that, for most people, navigating basic social interactions felt like moving through the forest at night without a torch.

And when things went wrong? It was never my fault. When I was kicked out of an appointment, my first instinct was to think: *What was their problem?*

But it began to dawn on me that I'd been ignorant. I'd been bashing my head against the wall, trying to get different results by behaving the same way.

I don't think we can change until we own our negative attributes and behaviors. I had a lot of poor habits. I was pretty negative by nature. I was and still am very easily frustrated. I always found an external factor for anything that went wrong in my life. It was never me.

But there was so much wrong: a lack of improvement in my field, my lack of growth in terms of my own agency, agents quitting on me, clients not buying from me, canceling on me, or not showing up for appointments. Could all of it really be purely their fault?

I wanted to succeed in my job, and something needed to change. I took Mike's words to heart and began working on my bedside manner.

Mike once told me that someone's reputation is never true or false. It's just what a bunch of people believe and what you hear commonly. Your own opinion of yourself can have little to do with your reputation. It's based on how your actions are perceived by others.

And my reputation wasn't the best in terms of the way I came off to people, treated people, or spoke to people.

My first instinct would be to say: "They took me wrong." But then I'd realize my delivery was awful, which had led them to view me in a different way than I truly meant. I often wasn't looking at things from others' perspectives.

I had to face it: I was thirty-seven years old and still just getting by. I had to own that. I started to look at myself in the mirror and ask: How did I contribute to this? How did I get here? What role did I play in the negative outcome?

Maybe I could have delivered something differently, maybe I could have approached someone differently, maybe I could have avoided a situation, maybe I could've had a better demeanor, maybe I triggered something in someone. I started to look at what I could change in any situation.

Maybe that guy who acted like a jack-off when he let me in his house didn't want the insurance; maybe his wife was pushing for it. So, I could've talked to her instead. That old lady might have offended me by implying that she felt unsafe around me, but would I be up for letting strangers into my house if I were in her position? And who cares where I make a sale—in the kitchen, the garage, on the roof—a sale is a sale. There's that saying again: "Do you want to be right, or do you want to be rich?"

If I took every sale that went bad and analyzed each and every one, I'd find a diversity of people, situations, lifestyles, moods, goals, dreams, and worries. But the common denominator in that list of failures was me.

And that was the one thing I had control over. That was the one thing I had ownership over.

I said that word over and over again in my head: *ownership*. So many times that the word broke up to form a new phrase that has become one of my mantras: Own. Your. Shit.

Ownership (noun): Own your shit

My first major breakthrough in reframing the way I communicated came from helping new recruits.

There was this new kid—let's call him Joe—who started at the office. In the introductory training sessions, he was saying all the right things. "I want to change my circumstances," "I wanna get rich," "I'm a go-getter," "I'm going to work hard," "I'm hungry," "I eat what I kill," you get the picture. He was full of piss and vinegar.

Brian showed me some texts he and Joe had passed back and forth. Brian had asked him how things went on his first day.

"Great," said Joe, "I made seventy calls."

"Good job," Brian replied. "Keep it up."

I was dumbfounded. Why would Brain just lie to him like that? Who was going to benefit from this kid getting the impression that these were remotely acceptable numbers?

I let Joe know I wanted a word with him the following day. It was simple. I was going to honestly tell him that those numbers were shocking.

"Bro, you're going to go broke," is how it usually would've started. "You're going to be out of this job in a week. Cut the shit. You want to make money like an adult, you have got to work like an adult."

But Brian's approach was still nagging at me. Why were we coming at things from such opposite ends of the spectrum? I mulled it over more and realized Brain was worried about retaining this guy. This job is so demanding and, at times, demoralizing for newbies that a decent chunk of them burn out or drop out in the first month. Brian was handling the guy with kid gloves so that he didn't run off.

And my approach? Coming down on him like a ton of bricks and making him feel awful? He might have learned the truth, but he also might have quit. And I did *truly* want him to succeed.

I started to wonder how many recruits might not have gone on to a better life because I'd treated them in a way they couldn't handle, and they quit.

I had to own that my delivery sucked. Deep down I want people to win, so I had to work on adjusting to different personalities. I could tell the truth—I just had to deliver it in a way that made it sink in. My thought process didn't have to change; I just needed more finesse in the way I communicated those thoughts.

There had to be a better approach, somewhere between Brian's carrot and my stick. I decided to try something new. Rather than telling Joe his performance absolutely sucked, I was going to make him arrive at this conclusion himself.

"So, it was your first day yesterday," I said to Joe when we sat down. "How many calls did you make?"

"About seventy," he replied confidently.

"Okay, let's talk about that. I'm gonna guess that out of those seventy calls, around sixty didn't answer, right?"

"Yeah, about that," Joe replied, wavering slightly; he'd likely started to see where this was going.

"And on average, how long does one single phone call take before it hits voicemail?"

"About thirty to forty-five seconds," said Joe.

"Well, let's round up to a minute for easy math, and it'll be doing you a favor," I said. "So, sixty calls at one minute each is how much time?"

"Sixty minutes," said Joe.

"Would you say the other ten calls took on average about three minutes each?" I asked.

"Mm-hmm," said Joe.

"So, we're up to about one-and-a-half hours working the phones yesterday," I said.

Joe looked at me. I was glad to see he wasn't getting defensive, or angry, or desperately searching for excuses—the usual reaction when I told someone they'd done a piss-poor job. It was more just…recognition.

"Yeah," he said. "That's not a good day's work."

You can't force a horse to drink. But leading him to water is better than beating the crap out of him. Instead of giving him hell, I allowed Joe to reach his own conclusions. And instead of getting defensive, he began to open up to me. The bravado fell away.

"I'm a little nervous about meeting people," he said. "I feel like I don't know the product enough. I don't think I'd know what to do when I got to their houses and had to talk to them."

This was a huge moment. I'd fully thought this guy saw himself as a hotshot able to get away with a bad work ethic and a worse attitude because the world owed him something. If I'd come at him hard, I wouldn't have found the real root of the issue. I wouldn't have been able to help him.

"I get it," I said. "But that's tomorrow's problem. Right now, you haven't booked a single appointment, so you don't even have to worry about how they will go just yet. Get good at the phones, and trust me, we'll make sure you're ready when the appointments come."

Sure enough, Joe went on to crush the phones that week and was off to the races.

I felt like I had developed a superpower. Not only had I gotten my point across, but I'd done it in a way where he felt understood; everyone had achieved the outcome they wanted.

Getting my point across—and being confident my words had not caused confusion—was everything.

I became obsessed with this new approach. I started stopping people halfway through a conversation to double-check we were on the same page. The number of times I'd hear "You're mad at me" or "I think you're being a bit rude" made me realize how much work I needed to do on my communication skills. But I was *happy* to do that work since it meant we were all moving closer to our goals.

During tricky interactions, I started letting people know that I was coming from a place of good faith, reinforcing that I had the best of intentions.

I started asking for feedback from people. It had to be from people I trusted—people who had shown levels of success in helping other people. And they let me know that I had to work on myself.

I knew when Mike told me about my bedside manner that it was Southern for "You're being an asshole." And I didn't want him to see me that way any longer.

I really care for the success of people in this business. And I felt like if I wasn't being honest and direct with people, I'd be lying. But my delivery was so bad, and I wasn't taking into account the way people learn or hear things. There had been such a big difference between what I said and what people heard.

Ten years on, and today, I am a different human being. As soon as I took ownership of my failings in certain situations and began the process of rectifying those mistakes, I was empowered.

It felt like the culmination of the movie *8 Mile*, where Eminem's character Jimmy (aka B-Rabbit) is in his final rap battle. He knows his rival has done his homework and found out about all the dysfunction going on in Jimmy's life—that he lives in a trailer with his alcoholic mother and her abusive boyfriend, that his girl cheated on him, that his friends are losers, and so on.

Instead of bracing for impact, waiting for this guy to tear him apart, Jimmy goes on the offensive, listing all of his own failings and referencing all of his own struggles.

Jimmy ends his turn with the lines, "I'm a piece of white trash, I say it proudly. Here, tell these people something they don't know about me."

His rival is stunned. Dumbfounded. All the ammunition had been used up, every weapon he'd hoped to fire off completely unloaded. In an extreme act of ownership of all his problems and personal failings, Jimmy had totally disempowered his opponent and snatched victory from the jaws of defeat.

I found the same freedom and empowerment when I admitted and faced my own failures. The day I realized I was the problem, I immediately became the solution. I had control over myself and my own actions.

Granted, I first practiced ownership of my problems in order to improve my numbers as a salesman; I'm not going to lie about that. My self-improvement was born out of selfishness. But the ultimate prize was when I saw how my new skills as a communicator made the lives of those around me better. Young recruits in the office were hitting their numbers and making money, getting on the path to creating better futures for themselves.

My family was sort of the final frontier for my transformation as a communicator, I'll be honest. At Thanksgiving, I always preferred to throw a baseball in the yard with the kids than shoot the shit with the adults in the kitchen. At dinner, I might have said nothing at all.

But my wife had seen me holding court at work events—she knew that I'd become a new man in my professional life. At a sales conference, I'd have a ring of people around me, and I wouldn't shut up, trying my best to add value to everyone around me. I'd learned what people responded to, what made them tick, and which parts of a talk worked and which didn't. I'd had time to assess which analogies and stories best got my point across, and I'd been able to hone these skills over time.

Sometimes, I felt like I was flying blind again outside of work. But Steph would help ground me since she'd seen the change I was capable of. And she wasn't going to let me off the hook, either, when we were at some type of other event outside of work.

"So, you know how to communicate at work, right?" she told me. "Why don't you give it a shot here?"

That was hard to argue with. I'd developed the skills to navigate the professional world, so why not choose to apply those same skills to my personal life?

Communicating as a high performer is difficult. It takes effort and finesse. Sometimes, when I leave the office, I want to switch off, but the people that I care about the most deserve the best from me.

If you put me in an environment with fifty insurance agents, you have to drag me out of the room. I can get on stage and let it rip. I'll engage with anyone, in complete comfort, now that I've learned how to get my points across. But I don't want to say three words around the Thanksgiving dinner table or at a school event full of other kids' parents. There's something wrong with that equation. I'm not perfect, but I'm working at it. I've owned that the problem is with me, and I'm the one that needs to fix it.

CHAPTER SEVEN
MISTAKES

By nature, I'm someone that's not afraid to make mistakes. I'm pretty comfortable messing things up. In fact, I'm all about making a mess of things and seeing what I learned from it.

There's a lot of people who are very timid when it comes to making mistakes. Some people call themselves perfectionists; they don't want to act until they've practiced and perfected something.

I think that's a really funny way to look at things. Imagine a footballer refusing to go onto the field until they were perfect at football. Imagine not wanting to start your next job until you are perfect at it. That makes no sense.

What if your kid tells you they don't want to play soccer because they're not perfect at it? What would you tell them? You'd tell them perfection doesn't exist. And if they are frustrated by making a mistake in practice, you'd say that's no reason to quit, it's a reason to persist.

Mistakes can be powerful, and they can really work for us. To get the most out of mistakes, I think it helps to face them with a four-pronged approach:

1. Be willing to make the mistake.

2. Own that you made the mistake.

3. Get feedback from someone that is better than you.

4. Implement what you were suggested to change.

You've got to be willing to put yourself in the position to fail—right in the middle of the fire. Not on the sidelines taking notes. You learn by doing, not by watching.

Did you learn how to ride a bike by watching your sibling? No. When you watch the Olympics on television, can you all of a sudden go out into the street and run one hundred meters in under ten seconds? Of course not. Did you feel comfortable getting in the water for the first time because you watched *Free Willy*? Didn't think so.

Sometimes, new agents will ask me if they can join me in the field because they are visual learners and will only pick stuff up if they see it in action. I say to them, that's not how it works. If you'd come along with me to my first appointment, you would have seen me totally bomb because, of course, it went poorly.

But now you want to come and join me on my 1,000th appointment, and you expect that you're going to be able to perform at my level because you were looking over my shoulder?

You have to be willing to get your hands dirty, make a fool out of yourself, and learn through trial and error. All that is good stuff. Expecting that you'll be able to run out there and execute flawlessly because you've seen someone else run a decent meeting is just a fairytale.

Next, you have to own that you made the mistake. If this sounds obvious or simple, then pal, you might not understand human nature as well as you thought. For most people, immediately shifting blame is a default reaction, almost a reflex.

Anyone who has kids will be aware that avoiding blame is second nature: "It's not my fault; it's their fault."

As sure as your knee will jerk after a doctor hits it with a little rubber hammer, the instinct to shift blame and responsibility is hardwired into us. We all need to make a stern effort to resist this impulse and own up to our mistakes. Otherwise, there's pretty much nothing separating us from toddlers.

Oftentimes, people will put their mistake down to circumstances, like fatigue, poor training, or a heavy workload.

But you know what's the absolute worst? Trying to shift blame onto another individual. Not only are you unwilling to admit your error, you are willing to take someone else down with you. Now, that is just cowardice, and I can't tolerate it.

You see it sometimes in sports. A soccer coach might spend the whole post-game press conference giving a referee hell for awarding a penalty kick that resulted in a three to two loss. Sure, maybe it was a bad call, but perhaps some analysis of the first two goals you let in is needed if we're truly to get to the bottom of why you suffered defeat.

I can't stand it when parents blame the umpire after a kids' baseball game. In my mind, I'm like, *we missed four ground balls; we got two hits all game; we absolutely sucked.*

I'm not saying we need to yell at the kids for messing up and make them feel bad. But an honest appraisal of what went well and what didn't go so well will lead to far more growth than shifting the blame onto the umpire, regardless of the questionable calls he may have made.

And that leads on to the third part of this approach: get feedback from someone who is better than you.

If I want to get better at golf, I can watch Tiger Woods on TV and pick up a few pointers on his swing. But how much am I going to actually improve my game?

Not much. Now, if I get *coached* by Tiger Woods, I think I'll make some pretty big strides.

Not being scared to ask for feedback from mentors—or those with more experience than you—is such an important trait. Chances are these people have made the very same mistake you just made, and they'll immediately know what you need to do in order to adjust and cut errors out of your process.

Oftentimes, if you are open to the suggestions of others, they'll let you know you've messed up before you are even aware an error was made; you'll have caught it so early that the damage is minimized.

The process of learning from people who are better than you never stops. When I was expanding from being an agent into running my own agency, I didn't have too much experience managing a team. I asked a friend of mine who ran his own business for his advice, and he said it's simple: "Management is about being honest about what you suck at, and then hiring people who are way, way better than you at those things."

Slowly but surely, I'm surrounding myself with people who are better than me in areas I'm weak in, and let me tell you, the results are unreal.

Now, it really is unfortunate that the fourth and final item in this list even needs to be addressed. But here we are. I've lost count of the number of times that I've given someone advice on some changes they need to make, only for them to go back out and keep doing the same thing.

Sometimes, it's because bad habits are hard to break, which I get. Sometimes, it's because people get stressed or absent-minded. But other times, I get the sense that people just think they know better. And that kind of arrogance is just not conducive to personal growth.

If you consistently ignore a mentor's advice, don't be surprised if they stop picking up the phone when you call.

CHAPTER EIGHT
OBSESSION

"If you want to get paid like a professional, you've got to act like a professional," Mike told me once, and these words have never been far from my mind ever since.

> *If you want to be paid like a professional, you better act like a professional*
>
> — *Mike Killimett*

Defining *professionalism* in a normal workplace is relatively straightforward, I'd say. The US Department of Labor has this to say:

"Professionalism does not mean wearing a suit or carrying a briefcase; rather, it means conducting oneself with responsibility, integrity, accountability, and excellence."

Which I'd agree with. But what happens when you get to a point where most people around you are conducting themselves along these lines? What separates you from the pack?

For me, it comes down to obsession. Elite level professionalism requires that you become obsessed with your profession. I think Kobe Bryant's leadership during the 2008 Olympics is the perfect example of this.

To set the scene, the US men's basketball team shocked the world by losing to Argentina in the semifinals of the 2004 Olympics. This was the first time the US men's team had not captured gold in the competition since the 1980s.

The failed campaign required a full-on post-mortem to try and determine how the most dominant force in Olympic basketball could fluff their lines in this way.

Some made excuses that the team was not at full strength, with stars like Shaquille O'Neal and Kobe Bryant staying home.

But the Americans hadn't exactly sent over a bunch of chumps. The team was stacked with ballers: a young LeBron James, Allen Iverson, Dwayne Wade, Tim Duncan, and Carmelo Anthony all traveled to the tournament.

A lot of commentators noted that the US had gotten cocky. They'd spent so long at the top that they hadn't noticed the other nations quietly making ground on them. The team simply hadn't prepared for the tournament. They'd thought that showing up would be enough, and it wasn't.

Fast-forward to the 2008 Olympics, and the pressure on the US team was palpable. The US players knew that anything less than gold would not cut it. Meanwhile, their competition now knew the Americans could be beaten; the aura of invincibility was gone.

That year's roster was dubbed "The Redeem Team," a nod to both the recovery task at hand and The Dream

Team—featuring Michael Jordan, Magic Johnson, and Charles Barkley—that took gold at the 1992 Olympics.

Stars from the ill-fated 2004 competition—including James, Wade, and Anthony—rejoined for the contest in Beijing. Wade and James went on to produce a Netflix documentary about the ultimately victorious campaign, in which the US had revenge over Argentina in the semi-final and defeated Spain to clinch gold in the championship game.

For my money, the documentary revealed what must have been a huge ingredient in the winning formula: the obsessive professionalism of team captain Kobe Bryant.

Bryant had been the obvious choice for the captaincy. His legendary Mamba Mentality had started all the way back in high school, where he woke up at 4:00 a.m. to shoot drills, giving him the jump on his teammates who joined practice at 8:00 a.m.

At first, the gains were only marginal. He was good, but not the best. But he kept at it—and eventually eclipsed his peers. Even so, he never abandoned his

4:00 a.m. starts. They stayed with him throughout his career.

Other players would say to him, "You don't need to wake up at 4:00 a.m. to practice drills; you're Kobe Bryant." They didn't understand that he was Kobe Bryant *because* of the 4:00 a.m. starts. His obsession with the game was what gave him his edge.

And it was this mentality that led the team to greatness. A group of supremely talented players could no longer rest on their laurels. Bryant demanded that they rise to the occasion and work harder than the competition. He led by example, and the team gelled as a cohesive unit, rather than a collection of individuals. He was more of a professional in that environment than the others were.

I have tried to emulate this mentality in my profession. What can I do to display elite professionalism in my work, even if I'm surrounded by people who are succeeding at a high level? Well, I try and do what they might not. That means getting in early. It means staying late. It means seeking advice from mentors at every turn, and it means responding to constructive criticism rather than rebelling against it.

In the movie *Hustle,* Adam Sandler's character plays a scout for the Philadelphia 76ers. He travels around the world looking for future stars of the NBA. To be clear, every player he looks at can play basketball. They can all handle the ball well, they all have decent shooting stats, they're all fast and strong. You or I wouldn't be able to identify what players would make it and which wouldn't, because what divides players at that level is miniscule.

Sandler's character is looking for the slightest edge, and sometimes it comes down to intangibles. When he gives his scouting report, he might point out that when someone talks trash, the player loses it mentally, and he's weak there, or perhaps he never shows up to practice early. The closer you rise to the top, the more success is decided by the finest of margins. And that's why you have to become obsessed with every last detail of how you handle yourself and your work.

When I see grown ass men shout at the TV during a football match because of a mistake a player has made, it makes me laugh. I wish they would put those same demands on themselves in their profession. I wish they applied those expectations to themselves—that they gave themselves hell when they fell short of perfection. Sadly, that's rarely ever the case. Most people are more willing to judge others before they judge themselves.

Realizing that checking in at 9:00 a.m. and clocking out at 5:00 p.m. would see me stay in place for the rest of my life and make no progress, I became obsessed with the process of getting better.

I became obsessed with discipline, with activity, with analyzing and learning from my mistakes. I became obsessed with tracking my progress and ensuring I was improving on my numbers incrementally, as well as constantly adjusting my goals upward.

I looked at it a lot like working out. If you want to get in ridiculous shape, it won't happen overnight. You have to commit to it day in and day out. Similarly, with professionalism, the better you do and the more you surround yourself with successful people, the harder it is to stand out.

If you are a beginner in the gym, you'll start to see results really quickly. If you go from never stepping in a gym to lifting weights three or four times a week and sticking to a high protein diet, you will get both physically and visibly stronger in a matter of months.

These "newbie gains" occur because your body is rapidly responding to these new stimuli, and your muscle synthesis is going into overdrive to accommodate this new active schedule.

But it doesn't last forever. After a while, your body gets used to this routine, and you'll add less and less muscle, despite sticking to the same schedule and diet.

In your first year of training as a beginner, you might gain up to two pounds of muscle a month. In your second year, you're lucky to gain one pound a month. And after four-plus years of training, you might expect to put on two to three pounds of muscle across the whole year.

In order to do even that, you have to work harder and become more obsessed, than you were at the beginning. You have to introduce something called "progressive overload," where you gradually increase the weight of repetitions in your routine over time.

You have to diligently monitor and track your work—as well as make minor adjustments, which end up being crucial in making gains. Whereas once you could rock up to the gym with very little planning and see incredible results, in an increasingly expert (or professional!) environment, you will only see improvements and set yourself apart from others by becoming obsessive about the details.

Repetition breeds improvement. So often, new recruits will come up to me and ask, "How do I deliver the perfect pitch?" And my answer is always the same: "I can't teach you that."

Or the long answer: The only way someone can improve your pitch is by attempting it a stupid number of times. By putting in the repetitions, you will grow in confidence and the process will become second nature. That is what people will respond to, not parroting something I've told you.

Plus, you have to respond to a volatile environment, like a golfer adjusting the angle of their shot due to the wind.

Every scenario is different, with different people, different emotions at play. There is no one-size-fits-all way of working with human beings, and the only way you are going to learn how to respond to individuals is by doing it over and over until you familiarize yourself with thousands of different scenarios that require thousands of different responses. I can't help you with that, and you can't train for that in front of the mirror in the bathroom. You've gotta get out in the field and get your hands dirty.

I started to get so many reps in, I stopped thinking and just acted out of muscle memory. If I got rejected or someone said something I didn't like over the phone, I didn't stutter; there were no longer long pauses; I was ready for it, and I knew exactly what to say to get back on track.

Things started popping when I went into this flow state. And I started to stand out. Management saw me studying, asking questions in training, and most importantly, implementing the stuff that was suggested. You'd be surprised how many people miss that last part. They want to appear vocal and active in training sessions by asking questions, but when it comes to acting on the advice, well, that's just too much work.

I became obsessed with going to events, connecting with the higher end producers in the trade. I was nonstop about improving my craft and learning from the best.

I think I naturally have an obsessive personality. If I start something, I get pretty locked in with it. I'm not the type of person who leaves a task incomplete very easily. Sometimes, I'll see my kids build half a tower out of Legos, get bored, and leave it laying on the floor half-done. I just can't relate to that. Whatever the task may be, I've always been like a dog with a bone.

I remember going down to the local arcade with my friend Brian. He would flit from one machine to the other—*Donkey Kong, Kirby, Street Fighter, Pacman*—sometimes abandoning a game midway through if it hadn't caught his attention or imagination enough. Meanwhile, I would sit on the same machine until one of three things had happened: I ran out of time, I ran out of quarters, or I'd achieved a high score.

And on the walk home, I would still be fully absorbed by the game, running through the various mistakes I'd made, figuring out how to come back stronger next time.

I've always been this way. Even now, I have to remind myself to be present during my leisure time. I can't count the number of times I've heard my wife try and snap me out of a trance—my body at home, my mind still in the office—"John? John? *John?* Where'd you go just then?"

I know a lot of people are capable of detaching themselves from their work. They leave on Friday evening, and boom, they won't think about their job until Monday morning. I simply cannot relate to that. I'm constantly thinking about what I need to do next, concerned that if I switch off then, I'm just going to come back to a chaotic mess.

Of course, it's important to find some balance in life, making time for your family and any pursuits outside the office that keep you happy and healthy. But I will not apologize for not switching off totally, and honestly, if I see my employees doing so, that's totally cool, but perhaps don't expect a promotion any time soon.

I like to monitor what I call the "give a shit level" in my office. This is different from the roles and responsibilities within the job description. Fulfilling those is pretty much the bare minimum. A high "give a shit level" means you've come in early or stayed late to complete a task to the best of your ability. It means you've taken the initiative and gone above and beyond when you've realized there's a better or more efficient way of doing something. It means you've taken time to help your colleague and acted as a collaborative team member if that's what it takes to complete a project ahead of schedule. It means you've sought out advice from your mentors and been inquisitive every step of the way, constantly looking to improve yourself and contribute to the mission.

If you have a high "give a shit level" and you mess up, it doesn't bother me. If you have a high "give a shit level," trust me, I will take care of you. I disproportionately reward my top people. I make it stupid unfair. My best people know how much I value them. Pay, perks, recognition, access, time, travel, whatever it is, I will go the extra mile for you if I see you going the extra mile in the workplace.

If other people in the office feel aggrieved, I make it clear that the situation is entirely of their own making. That is because I judge people against the standard that they have created for themselves.

I won't set targets for people. I will ask people what they want to achieve. What do they think is a reasonable level of work? What goals do they think they should strive for? What is attainable? What are they going to bring to the table to justify their hire?

And I make sure to make note of these goals. Every last detail. And I tell them what I'm doing; it's totally transparent.

"You are telling me this is what you're going to do for me," I will say. "Let's be clear. I have asked nothing of you. You have assigned yourself these goals. Therefore, if you fail, you cannot say that I gave you unrealistic targets."

This method holds people accountable for their own shit. It also removes the possibility of a sh*tty attitude or victim mentality. If you fail, you have to have a chat with yourself about what went wrong. You can't blame anyone else.

Taking initiative and applying yourself are both big parts of professionalism. The number of times I get bugged by people looking for answers they can find on their own...it's a lot. I welcome people coming to me with queries and problems, but there needs to be a personal vetting process before you come to me. It starts something like this: Can this question easily and obviously be answered without bothering John? If the answer is no, come to me! If the answer is yes, I'll see you next time.

In life insurance, agents have to familiarize themselves with a range of products—maybe up to ten products at any one time. With dozens of recruits and multiple products, if I sat down and answered every question that came my way, I'd have no time left in the day to get anything else done.

So, I ask agents: if you were able to study a product nonstop, how long would it take you to learn it inside-out? Sometimes the answer is a few hours, sometimes a day—one guy even told me a week.

So, let's say it takes you a week—which is definitely too long, but for the sake of argument, we'll say it takes ten weeks to learn every product we have inside-out.

After which, you can never ask me a product question again in your career. Sound good?

An agent will say, "Yeah, I guess."

And I'll respond, "You've been here two years, and you're still asking me basic shit? What are we doing?"

After a few months, I just wouldn't understand why; at the very least, it's clear you don't know where to get the information. That lack of intuition and initiative is concerning.

If you're a loan officer, and you're writing different mortgage products, how do you not know them after a few months?

This is a surefire way to weed out those who are professional and those who are not; those who are obsessed and those who are not. Who has engaged and taken the time to master the material, and who is still asking basic questions after years on the job?

There's an old story from the music industry that I think demonstrates this perfectly. American rock band Van Halen used to have this odd demand in their concert rider, which was the document they would send over to the booker relating their requirements for the performance. Singers have a list of demands in their riders. Mariah Carey allegedly requires two dozen white roses. Drake reportedly needs incense burning at all times in his trailer.

But Van Halen's request seemed particularly bizarre. The band asked for a bowl of M&M's with the stipulation: *WARNING—absolutely no brown ones.*

At the time, the band was taking one of the most technically advanced shows ever around the US. There were pyrotechnics, enormous lamp lights, and heavy moving parts all over the stage. If things weren't set up right, someone could get badly injured or worse.

So, the removal of the brown M&M's? It wasn't some diva-ish demand. If the band got backstage and saw the bowl of candy excluding the brown variety, they could be assured that the booker had read and adhered to every detail in the rider. If they arrived to find the brown candy in the bowl, or worse still, no M&M's altogether? The band would request a thorough line check of the entire stage to make sure it was safe to go out.

So, when an agent comes to me and asks a question—the answer to which has been sitting for a year in an unopened training file on their desktop—I know right away: this guy is serving me brown M&M's. They haven't read the material, and I should be seriously concerned over their commitment.

It's the same with learning a phone script. If my thirteen-year-old son can memorize a whole Bible verse for school in one week, you, a thirty-something-year-old professional, can learn a phone script after three months.

It may seem like I'm being harsh or lacking sympathy, but you know what? Too bad. Sometimes, the tasks that aren't met are so simple there can't be any other explanation: you just didn't put the effort in.

Now, if I see you trying really hard at something difficult, and you absolutely suck? I will be right behind you. I will give you everything I've got to get us both over the line. I just have to know you are trying; otherwise, you're on your own.

CHAPTER NINE
RESILIENCE

What do the radio, stainless steel, computer, printing press, Wi-Fi, and Bluetooth all have in common? They were all game-changing inventions born out of a time of crisis.

Times of widespread disease, economic downturn, and war are defined by human suffering. But these are also times when innovative people can shine. Seeing a crisis as an opportunity for growth is one of the things that has helped me most in business—and life.

A lot of us use adversity as an excuse for bad performance. A rough patch validates why we're not having some level of success. We tell ourselves that's okay.

But here are two simple truths:

1. Someone else's shit is always worse than your shit.

2. Anyone can perform during good times. Successful people perform during bad times too.

That first truth is all about perspective. It's not to say you shouldn't dwell on what's gone wrong in your life. It's important to reflect. And it's okay to compare your situation to another person's. As long as your takeaway is "Things could be worse" and not "I have it worse than them."

One of the core values in my office is resilience. I define this as "the capacity to recover quickly from difficulties."

Sometimes, putting your difficulties in perspective can help in this regard. I encourage people to be open about their problems. And boy, do people like to talk about their problems—that part is easy!

I remember a chat I had with a recruit; let's call him Kevin. He was not even close to where he should have been, performance-wise. The number of calls and appointments he was making...you couldn't even describe it as "part-time," more like insurance was a casual hobby.

The thing that was so funny about this conversation was that Kevin treated it as a foregone conclusion that there simply wasn't room for improvement.

I asked Kevin what he thought he might be able to do to improve his numbers (and it had taken me a while to phrase it like that; I'd used to simply ask, "Why do you suck so much?"). His response was matter-of-fact.

"Oh, I have another part-time job two days a week, and I have to pick up my kid on Fridays. It's not possible to get my numbers up."

"Do you know Jennifer?" I asked him, referring to another recruit.

"Sure," he said.

"Did you know that Jennifer is a single parent with three kids, and that she works another job three days a week?" I asked.

"Okay…" Kevin said. He could probably see what was coming.

"Well, Jennifer doubled your call volume last month," I said. "Now, I'm not saying you need to be like Jennifer. Not everyone can. But I *would* say Jennifer provides us with some valuable context."

I wasn't trying to shame Kevin here. I was trying to show him that he'd gotten stuck in a mental rut, convincing himself that his circumstances were such that he couldn't possibly grow or improve. When he was provided with the comparison of an individual who was excelling and from a more disadvantageous starting point…well, if that's not going to shake you out of that rut, nothing will.

The first step in helping Kevin come to this realization was getting him to be honest about his problems. You need to be honest and communicative to gain valuable perspective.

I encourage people to be open and transparent about their problems; that way, we can help each other, relate to each other, and above all else, build a thick skin through witnessing each other's resilience.

I've been through a lot. I grew up piss-poor, was a teenage dad, and had four kids before I was thirty. I lived paycheck to paycheck most of my life, had two houses foreclosed on, went bankrupt, got divorced and struggled with a damaging combination of alcohol and antidepressants.

Do you know what helped me recover from this and grow into the person I am today? Witnessing others in far worse circumstances display far greater resilience. I didn't know it at the time, but one of those people was my mother.

I remember when I was eight years old going to the convenience store across the road to buy packs of cigarettes. If I'd used cash, the guy probably wouldn't have sold them to me. But since I pulled out food stamps—along with a scrawled note from my mom—the cashier didn't bat an eye.

I grew up in Lynn, a small city between Boston and Salem along the coast of Massachusetts. Half the people I've told this don't know where the hell Lynn is. The other half spout off the opening line to the infamous jingle dedicated to town:

Lynn, Lynn the city of sin
You never come out, the way you came in

You ask for water, but they give you gin
The girls say no, yet they always give in

If you're not bad, they won't let you in
It's the damnedest city I've ever lived in

Lynn, Lynn the city of sin
You never come out, the way you came in.

They say that the rhyme was cooked up by sailors during Prohibition who would come over from the port in Boston looking for bootleg liquor and prostitutes.

One of the mayors in the nineties tried to change the name of the city to Ocean Park, believing that the song was stopping people from moving to Lynn for work or leisure.

Lynn was historically known as "the city of firsts" because of all the groundbreaking industry that went on there, like the creation of America's first jet engine.

When I grew up there, manufacturing had been on the decline across the region for years, and the place was what you'd call "rough around the edges." We grew up in the projects, and there was a bunch of crime. There were gangs and drugs; it wasn't somewhere you wanted to go on purpose.

My mom's strong desire was to get us out of there from the get-go, but it became a matter of urgency when I got to junior-high age. Things got pretty heavy in public school around that age. That's when fights started putting kids in hospitals and thieves leveled up from candy to cars.

Up until that point, my mom had been attending community college and living off welfare, since it paid better than pretty much any job she was qualified for at the time. When she finished her studies, the college gave her a job with a decent salary, and she sent me off to a Catholic junior high school. I now understand the amount of planning, work, savings, and effort that went into my mother getting us out of the projects.

By remembering that time, I can tap into perhaps one of the greatest lessons in resilience I could wish for. A teenage mom, a dad who was never around much, and two kids, living in the projects somewhere in the armpit of Boston and Salem.

It was cheaper to live off welfare and food stamps than to support us on a minimum-wage job. You could have forgiven her for never getting us out of that situation. But she was resilient. There was nothing *woe is me* about her. She could have blamed the system or the people who had put her in that position, but she chose to work her way out of it. She knew she needed training to earn a wage that would be large enough to support my brother and me *plus* taking us out of Lynn. She used her computer programming degree and leveraged it into a job on campus in Beverly.

She did all of this with pretty much no support. My parents got married when I was four and divorced within the year. I'm not sure why they busted up exactly. I remember him drinking hard. When I was around ten years old, he would come pick me up for visits to his place in Rhode Island for the weekend. The first stop was always his favorite local bar, where I'd spend the night playing pool and eating out of a giant jar of maraschino cherries the bartender would give me. It felt like the TV show *Cheers*, where everyone knew my name, except I was a little kid.

Anyhow, getting back to the divorce, I got the sense that my mom might have walked in on him with someone else or seen him doing something pretty stupid. Our departure was rather abrupt. My aunt came to pick me up and take me back by train to Lynn from my dad's place in Rhode Island, where we had briefly moved. My mom packed up all our shit and left one of every essential item for him: one fork, one knife, one cup, one plate, and so on. Single items for a newly single man.

After that, he was pretty much gone. I'd see him every now and then—the odd weekend here or there for a trip to McDonald's, the ballpark, or to visit his mom. But he did not make much of an effort to be in our lives. We bounced around between family members—my aunt and grandfather—until we settled in at the Neptune Towers apartment building in Lynn.

Sometimes, if I acted stupid, my mom would call my dad up to yell at me. I never understood why. Of all people, why would I care what that guy had to say? I saw him once in a blue moon in his crappy apartment, where there was only out-of-date Raisin Bran to eat and nowhere to go because his shitty car was broken down again. And I'm getting lectured by this guy? Nah, I'll skip the lesson, thanks. My mom stopped making those calls after a while.

When I got a family of my own, I had such a desire to keep a stable family unit going—and not be like my dad—that I ended up sticking around longer than I should have in my first marriage.

Things got rocky between my first wife Jamie and I. And while I loved our daughter, I didn't love being married. So, my stupid solution was to have *more* children (four in total) rather than addressing the problems within my relationship head-on through communication.

Eventually, those problems came to a head, and it was too much. I gave up. I left. I walked out, just as my dad had done. I was imitating the very man I'd tried desperately to be better than. My oldest son was eight at the time and was distraught. He has not quite forgiven me for that to this day. History repeating itself.

I did pretty much everything I could to handle the situation poorly. No resilience whatsoever. I was a piss-poor communicator and kept Jamie in the dark about how I was feeling. I was taking Lexapro, an anxiety and depression medicine and drank way too much vodka. History repeating itself.

It was Steph who saved me. She supported me while I was bankrupt and hashing out child support and divorce in court. She helped me when I had a car taken away and two houses foreclosed on. She took one look at the way I was numbing myself on Lexapro and immediately came up with a plan to wean me off the stuff.

In a few months, I felt like a normal person again. I had been living in a daze for years. I realized how much the drug had numbed me to the world. I had been moving through life with such…apathy.

Steph was a glass-half-full person, and I still hadn't rid myself of my half-empty attitude.

We moved in together, got married in 2010, and had Maddox a year later. I was working in a spa at the time and picked up some insurance work on the side a few years later. I remember sitting at a folding table in Steph's garage with my phone in front of me. I was full of nerves and frustration, scared to dial the numbers. Steph would pour me a glass of vodka OJ. Maybe it was the liquid courage, or having her there, or a bit of both. But soon I started making calls, and I felt invincible; the *nos* would bounce off me like nerf bullets on a suit of armor.

I quit the spa job in 2013 and committed to insurance full-time. I was away from home a whole lot. And when I was home, I had to adjust to no longer being the center of Steph's world. I was once again in a married-with-children situation.

I had taken advantage of her willingness to support me, and when that dynamic changed, I freaked out. In late 2017, I bolted again. Once more, I took the easy way out and just left. And the worst part? Just months earlier, Steph had been diagnosed with cancer. She worked a full-time job and took care of a kid through all of it. She would go to radiation treatment on her lunch break. She had surgery and barely took any time off.

I was grinding away, getting my numbers up, maniacally committed to never being broke again in my life. Meanwhile, she was working her ass off, too, while keeping death at bay. What was I doing? How was I letting this person slip through my fingers?

She filed for divorce, but we never went through with it. The door was left ajar for some kind of reconciliation. We were seeing other people when I texted her.

Can we talk about fixing this instead of splitting it all up? I wrote.

I didn't deserve it, but she gave me a second shot. She worded it way better than me:

"It would be easier to walk away from each other than it is to commit to staying in a marriage and working on it. Let's not take the easy way out."

She had suggested couples therapy just before our separation, and I had refused. If it takes things like therapy, you just shouldn't be together, right?

But then I realized everything good and worthwhile takes work. The more work you put in, the better you are for each other. If you're not working, you're not trying, and if you're not trying, you're an awful partner to be with.

I thought, *Jeez. I'm the guy who spends his life at work teaching people how to fix things and find solutions to problems. And at the first sign of problems in my relationships, I shut down or peace out?* Something is wrong with this equation.

When Steph and I got back together, I begged her to come to therapy with me, and she appeased me. I didn't want to go alone; it reminded me of being put in therapy by my mom when I was seven or eight, and I hated it.

It was in therapy that I learned how much resentment Steph had built toward me. There's her constant support and willingness to handle everything for us. Then, when Maddox comes along and our routine changes, I grow sulky and distant. The imbalance there was so obvious, but I only truly understood it when she was able to say it out loud—and that only happened once we started communicating and stopped fighting.

So, while I was trying to grow an insurance agency, she and I set out to try and repair something that was broken. I still had to run the business. She still had to work. We still had to take care of the kids.

We still had to keep a smile on our faces. Most of our friends and family didn't realize what we'd been going through.

Of course, many couples have gone through worse. But I've certainly seen people stop trying at the sign of smaller obstacles.

One of the things that I learned from Steph is to look back on a particularly difficult part of your life. Say you lost a job, or you had a bad break-up, or you had an illness.

Think hard about what you went through to get past that period. Think about the resilience you showed, the determination, the grit. Think about how proud you are to have survived that and become the person you are today.

Now, faced with your current problem, visualize yourself in the future, on the other side of it, looking back at the strength you showed to make it out the other side once more.

The problems of the present—just like the problems of the past—can lead to growth and positive outcomes.

Give yourself one imaginary second, as if you are already in the future and have received a positive outcome, and you may even become grateful for the adversity. Sitting around and sulking isn't going to help.

Steph and I now spend a lot of time helping other couples through difficult situations, and it's not because we have this perfect marriage. It's precisely because our marriage was imperfect—and still, we soldiered on—that I believe we're qualified to give this type of support.

We do it because we like to be honest and transparent about our struggles, so we can help other people navigate through tough times.

If it hasn't become obvious by now, when I talk about resilience in this chapter, I'm not talking about myself. I'm talking about the most resilient people I have ever known, my mother and my wife. Through them, I have learned what grit and determination look like.

My mom taught me I didn't have to settle for a shitty life. That no matter what cards I'd been dealt, I could win the game, as long as I didn't feel sorry for myself and put the work in.

Steph taught me that no matter how bad you think you've got it, there is always someone worse off than you.

"How did you do it?" I asked her once. "How did you manage it all?"

"It was simple," she said. "Every time I went to the cancer ward, I saw a dozen people who were sicker than me. If they could do it, what reason did I have to fall to pieces?"

Steph is a pretty positive person. I'm not. I'm pretty negative. If you are like me, get yourself around someone positive and compare your situation to others. There are probably people—no matter what your situation is—that would kill to be where you are. Because there's always someone worse off. So, don't let your own shit slow you down.

When things had gotten hard in life, I'd been a runner, just like my dad. Repairing things with Steph allowed me to break the cycle of running away. With the resilience I've now learned, history doesn't have to repeat itself.

CHAPTER TEN
EXPECTATIONS

Think back to a time you were frustrated. About anything. You've got beef with a friend. Your mom has pissed you off. Your brother let you down. Most of the time, I bet you're frustrated because you expected something different out of a situation—and that expectation turned out wrong.

So, in a way, aren't *you* causing the frustration, if your expectations are behind the whole situation? Now, I'm not saying that what the person did to you was right or wrong; that's not my place. But I know I don't get as frustrated if I'm realistic about what I can expect from someone.

It's a fine line. I find I have to be careful about my expectations. I'm not saying I shouldn't have them.

But I have noticed that many of my frustrations in life came from having unrealistic expectations of people or situations.

> **Expectations:** premeditated way to create disappointment.
>
> —Inky Johnson

Conversely, there may have been times in my life when my expectations of myself were too low.

I tell my agents all the time: if you go to a restaurant and order a medium steak and it comes out well-done, would you get frustrated with the chef? Of course you would. That is an entirely reasonable expectation to have. Now, do you get mad at yourself when you don't work the way you said you would? When you don't perform well in your career, do you get as mad at yourself as you do at the cook who messed up your steak?

Learning to adjust my expectations of others has been a big personal stress reliever.

I used to expect that my agents all performed to the level that I did, but that is unreasonable. Instead of staying mad, I have readjusted my expectations.

Now, I simply expect three things from my agents: 1) that they are coachable, 2) that they do what they say they are going to do, and 3) that if they can't do number two, they communicate with me. However, there can only be so many number threes.

These are very simple expectations. And if you don't meet them, I'm not mad, I'm just out. We're done. I will quit you before you quit me.

The psychologist Samantha Young has helped me identify a list of dangerous expectations that can negatively impact life. She calls her following expectations "Happiness Killers"[7]:

- **That life should be fair.** It's not; shit happens, deal with it.

---

7   https://humanpsychology.com.au/expectations-the-real-hapiness-killer/

- **That everyone should like me.** I made peace with this one a long time ago. I can be a real asshole, so I really shouldn't expect to be universally adored.
- **That people should agree with me.** This was a big one for me. Learning to stop being frustrated when people didn't act on my advice has been an uphill battle.
- **That people understand what I am saying.** Dear lord, tell me about it. It took me a while to realize that what I say and what people hear are often two *totally* different things.
- **That I must always do well.** Realizing I just needed to be persistent instead of perfect was the foundation of my success.
- **That things will make me happy.** It is a very strange phenomenon that people often suck at predicting what will bring them happiness. Really think about this one the next time you are considering that sports car.
- **That I can change people.** There is precisely one human being you have the power to change in this world—and that is yourself.

Now, let's look at things from a different perspective. What happens if you exceed my expectations? *Man will I take care of you.* I spoil my people. I can be a real prick a lot of the time, but if you stick with me and show me loyalty—if I can *rely* on you—you will be rewarded.

Take my employee Amanda for example. I hired her when she was nineteen years old, not long out of high school. She was an assistant's assistant on thirty thousand dollars a year.

Seven years in, she's Director of Operations making $150,000 a year. She stays in plush hotels across the country when we go to events. When I travel with the team, everyone else goes coach, and she rides up in first class with me.

I love to reward the people that have shown me loyalty and effort. If you fail or make a mistake, if your intentions were good and it's obvious that you're trying, then I will be super forgiving.

In fact, you have to really pay attention to an employee's body of work before judging them by their mistakes.

Because odds are, the more work you do, the more you'll mess up.

Let's say Tom and Jerry are practicing three-pointers over a two-week period. Tom makes three hundred out of one thousand shots in his first week, while Jerry makes forty out of one hundred. The next week, Tom makes four hundred out of one thousand, and Jerry hits forty-five out of one hundred. Over the course of the two weeks, Tom has missed over one thousand more shots than Jerry. But he's worked way harder, and as a result he's improved his average. Tom is the guy you want on your team.

Now, there is a third type of individual who is the absolute worst. That guy won't even practice. He'll come up with excuses why he couldn't shoot hoops that day. Or he'll come up to you and badger you with questions without actually putting the work in:

"How should I stand before I shoot? Where should my elbow be? Should I hold my breath? Should I look at the ball or the basket?"

Some of these questions are smarter than others, but all are irrelevant if you're not putting the practical time in on the court.

Fortunately for me, Amanda put the work in from the word *go*. She used her intuition and was a total self-starter. She also puts up with me and my shit, which is no small feat.

I love to spoil Amanda, and while my treatment of her may act as an incentive to others in the office, that's not why I do it. I love to be a provider for people I care about, whether it be my kids, my wife, my most loyal employees, or my greatest friends.

And I think perhaps that was a large motivator behind my journey toward financial security and professional success. I was maniacally selfish for a period of time to get myself to where I needed to be, all the while knowing that the ultimate goal was to share my eventual riches.

I was out on the road most of the week and didn't really have a marriage for long stretches, but knowing that I was setting up my marriage and family for long-term comfort and prosperity—that made it bearable.

I have had a high employee turnover in the past because I am demanding. I have limited patience for people who are whiny and needy. I want you to justify your place within the ecosystem of the business. I don't want to hold your hand. The company does not exist to support you. Your role exists to make money for the company.

I'm not trying to be an asshole, but I've had times during staff meetings when I've looked around the room and thought, *My goodness, if I stopped paying half of you, this company would net more money.* That is how a business owner has to think sometimes, and I think the sooner an employee realizes that, the sooner they can adopt a perspective, attitude, and work ethic that makes them invaluable.

If you can't show me how you are adding value and making money for me, our relationship has a limited shelf life. Conversely, if you make my job easier, and it's apparent that you are making money for the company in excess of your salary? Then I have all the time in the world for you.

I used to be so much worse than I am now. I would get frustrated at not being able to articulate my ideas.

I would lose my shit over the smallest things—if a meeting didn't go exactly how I wanted it, if a video conference link hadn't been sent to me on time, and so on. The most trivial shit would send me over the edge. And Amanda would maintain her cool, keep perspective for the both of us, and guide us through tricky moments.

I don't know if it's because she knew I was always coming from a good place—and that snapping was a symptom of the pressure I was under—or if she had an unusual capacity to withstand bullshit. Maybe she just really needed the job.

It was probably a combination of all of those things. I have to say, I did adopt an intentional strategy of overpaying her so she didn't quit. She stuck by me, and hopefully, she's in a position now where it all seems worthwhile. On my end, I want her with me going forward, whatever it is I end up doing.

If I packed up my life insurance business and struck off to run an ice cream stand, I'd want her right next to me. Why? Because she'd take initiative and figure out how to get shit done without needing my direction. And if she saw that you, my new ice cream sales recruit, were slacking? She'd take you to task before I had a chance to.

I hate micromanaging people; it's my least favorite thing ever. This might surprise some people who have worked for me in the past, who might've felt micromanaged. Well, guess what? I didn't *want* to do it; it's just that you sucked at completing your daily tasks, so I had to get on your case.

Just the other day, I opened up a spreadsheet in a shared folder and noticed that it hadn't been updated like I'd agreed upon with an employee. In fact, the employee had stopped updating this particular spreadsheet weeks back. I called them into my office.

"Why haven't you been updating the spreadsheet like we agreed?"

"Oh, yeah, I figured we didn't need to keep doing it."

"What made you think that?"

"Well, I didn't see a reason to keep up with it."

"Let me get this straight. First of all, you need to be given a convincing explanation behind every single thing I ask you to do, otherwise you won't do it? And second, I now have to dedicate the rest of my day to figuring out what other shit you've simply stopped doing?"

It really boggles the mind. And it's not that I don't appreciate that there might be a better way of doing something. Present it to me, and I'm all ears.

Let's say that one of your jobs each day is to come into the office and move a glass of water from one table on one side of the room to a table on the other side of the room. Every day, that's one of your tasks.

If I come in and you've stopped doing the task, no matter how mundane or meaningless it appears, it automatically tells me that you have the wrong attitude. You're telling me that because you are bored of the task or because you don't understand why it needs to be done, you are simply going to stop doing it, despite getting money from me each month.

Now, I'm not asking you to be a mindless drone and simply carry out tasks without being inquisitive. That's not it at all. If you continue to move the water from one side of the room to the other and come up to me, saying, "Hey, boss, clue me in as to why this is important, so perhaps I can find a better way of staying on top of it," then I'm with you.

If I come in the next day and you personally haven't touched the water, but you've designed a contraption that does it for you automatically? High-five.

I just don't want to be coming to you in three months being like, "Hey, about that water thing, it appears to still be on one side of the room," and hear you say, "Oh yeah, I stopped doing that ages ago, it seemed pointless to me."

And if the task hasn't been completed because you forgot? Okay; what system do you have in place to ensure this doesn't happen again? Do you have a checklist? Is it on a whiteboard or on your laptop or scribbled on the inside of your eyelids? It better be *somewhere,* and it better be pretty much foolproof from here on out. Because I am not a kindergarten teacher. I don't want to make sure that you've cleaned up after yourself and that you've eaten properly and that you've dressed appropriately for the weather. I don't want to check your diaper. In other words, I don't want to have to remind you of the tasks that make up the bare minimum of your workday.

In case you haven't picked it up by now, I'm not the kind of boss that is going to congratulate you on doing your job. I'm not going to give positive reinforcement when things run as they should. I'm not going to pat you on the back when you've fulfilled what is mandated in your contract.

Now, if you go above and beyond and find some way to blow your targets out of the water, make or save my company a bunch of money? Man, I'll take you out for a steak dinner and cut you a fat bonus. Accolades and praise are reserved for extraordinary achievements. There are no participation trophies in Corporate America. Do not get it twisted. Politically correct office culture may have fooled you into thinking you are a unique and precious snowflake. But that is not the case. We live in a cutthroat, dog-eat-dog society, and the sooner you recognize that and grow a thick skin and sharp teeth, the better.

If I hire you, and after six months the company is growing at the same rate as before you arrived, that's a problem, my guy. It means I'm losing money on your salary. You have not justified your role within this organization. That has to be clear from the get-go. You are basically starting in a deficit, and you have to play catch-up. Look at it this way: making back your salary is a prerequisite for keeping your job.

Now, if you do that, and *then* some? If you help make the company grow? Well, you're going to see some of that end up in your bank account on top of your salary. It's a very simple equation. But me spending time answering all your questions and hearing all of your complaints as I pay you a salary, only for you to contribute nothing to the growth of the company? That math doesn't check out.

If you can't make this easy on me, I will find someone else because there's 300 million people in the country.

Make sure to pay attention to the revenue my company is making. If it goes up, that's good. If it goes down, that's not good. It's surprising to me how many employees will be unaware of the prospects of the company as a whole. But if I am late putting your paycheck in, that'll get noticed right away.

That is why there is such high turnover in this industry. Most people don't want to put the work in. They want to do the bare minimum. There is so much money in this industry, and it is populated by so many broke agents—broke simply because they are not putting in the work.

It's a bit like going to the gym the first week of January. You're going to see a whole bunch of people working out. But not everyone is jacked.

For most of my life, I was a scrawny little sucker; you could see my ribs. I was in my early thirties when I first started doing CrossFit, and when I got up to 190 pounds, and I was excited.

I got into insurance around five years later, and I just gave up. I wasn't taking care of myself anymore. I was on the road so much, sitting in my car for hours, not moving, eating a bunch of drive-through junk food. A Chick-fil-A Spicy Deluxe Sandwich, two large fries, and a large lemonade. That was lunch for many days—and sometimes dinner. For five years.

I got fat. Up to 250 pounds. I'm 6'1", so I probably held it better than most, but I remember seeing a picture one day, and I was slouched over, my gut hanging way over my pants. I thought: *That's the nastiest thing I've ever seen.* I still have that picture, and to this day, it provides me with motivation.

There was another time when I was at home with Maddox. He was probably six or seven, and I couldn't keep up with him in the yard. I was wheezing. I struggled to bend down and tie my shoe. I was a total mess, man.

I remember it hit me. What changed in my professional life was that I had set expectations of myself. I was going to commit to a schedule. I was going to meet my targets. I was going to make my phone calls, even though I didn't want to do it. I was going to stay consistent; I was going to be the first in the office just to prove a point. I set these expectations for myself and held myself accountable.

If I am already that person, why don't I just set the same standards and expectations for my health and physique? Why don't I remain consistent and hold myself accountable? Why don't I lift something heavy or sweat every day, and not be a fatass?

I didn't like being unable to run around with my kids. I didn't like how I looked or how I felt. I had lied to myself that this was simply part of my new commitment to work—that I just didn't have time to work out or eat healthy. But that, of course, was total bullshit. No matter how hard you work, you can always find a way to get exercise.

One day, I just woke up and thought, *I'm done.* I refuse to hold such low expectations of myself. Shortly after one Christmas, I started doing intermittent fasting. I only ate between noon and 8:00 p.m., and I didn't change my diet at all. I lost twenty pounds doing that in three months. Eating Oreos and ice cream at 7:59 pm.

Then I started watching what I ate and cutting out junk food, and I got down to 199 pounds right at the end of the year.

I was skinny, and I had no muscle. I was oddly shaped and felt uncomfortable. I started following fitness industry entrepreneur Andy Frisella, who gave me the attitude adjustment I needed. He's a hardass who will tell you exactly what you need to hear, no matter how much it sucks to acknowledge. I also noticed an acquaintance from the insurance space was posting about Frisella's program "75 hard"—and he was getting jacked, unreal results.

The way it works is this. You must:

- Follow a diet
- Perform two 45-minute workouts each day (one of which has to be outdoors)
- Drink one gallon of water a day
- Read ten pages of a non-fiction book
- Take a progress photo
- Avoid alcohol and no cheat meals
- Do all of the above for 75 days

The diet can be of your choosing, but you must stick to it closely and cut out alcohol.

Finally, and most brutally: you cannot make any alterations to the program. If you break any of the above rules, your progress resets to day one.

So, I'm watching this insurance guy I know do this and get jacked—literally transform himself. The first time I saw the program, I was fat as hell, and I was like, there's no way I can do all that; it's too much.

Then, on Christmas 2020, I rolled out of bed (for some reason I seem to prefer Christmas resolutions to the New Year variety) and thought: *I'm doing it. I'm going to take it seriously this time.* I started 75 Hard on December 26, 2020.

I've done it three times now. And dude, I've gotten ripped from the discipline of it. The thing is, the individual tasks in 75 Hard aren't necessarily difficult in isolation. But taken together, they require extreme focus and discipline, especially around travel, vacations, shitty weather, snowstorms, sick kids, you name it.

For me, it all came down to expecting enough from myself. Expecting that I was going to follow through with what I said I would.

We all know what it takes to lose weight and exercise. There is a multibillion-dollar industry based on helping people get there with any number of cheats and shortcuts. But at the end of the day, no one is confused. If you stick to healthy food—chicken, fish, veggies, and rice—drink plenty of water, and work out a lot, you're going to look fantastic. It's super simple, but not many people do it, or at least stick with it.

For me, the expectation was that I would stick to the plan. There was zero chance that I was going to commit to something and not do it. None.

I remember the first time I did it, I went to a cigar lounge and then a bar with a few buddies, watching them get tipsy as I sipped on water.

Keep in mind, I actually like to drink. A lemon-drop martini is my drink of choice. (Feel free to make fun of me, but please try one; you won't regret it. I've got all my friends hooked on them.) Sitting in that bar and not drinking took discipline at first, but eventually, I got used to it. My expectation was that if I knew the outcome would be preferable, I could commit to the discipline of it. I was going to do it every day.

And it worked well. I'm forty-seven at the time of writing this and in the best shape of my life. I've been on a four-year health journey, and I've been super consistent. Very few people remember the old, fat John. This is who I am now.

When people meet me, they assume this is how I've been my whole life—in the same way they might assume that the financial success I've had has always been there. I always have to explain that they missed the fat, lazy, broke bum.

This is part of the reason I try not to make assumptions when dealing with my agents. I don't know what their situation is. I'm not sure where they are coming from.

So, I ask a lot of questions. And it's more out of curiosity than to trip people up. If you say to me you can only run a few appointments a week, that you've got another job, that you have stuff going on, I won't care at all. But understand that your returns are going to be really inconsistent—especially in this industry, where there are chargebacks, and clients cancel.

If you sell three applications this month and book a Disney vacation, what are you going to do when two of those three clients cancel, and you are negative next month? How are you going to handle that?

Or is 100% of your insurance money going into a savings account that you are not going to touch? I need to ask a lot of questions to figure out the situation that we are dealing with. Who are you? What's your plan?

If you say your plan is to run three meetings a week and get rich, bro, you need to alter your expectations. If you say you want to earn an A-plus income and give me C-minus work, I'll get frustrated as hell. If you are happy with a C-minus income, then high-five, that's fantastic, but don't complain to me when rent is due.

Now, I started part-time. I can relate fully. I had a job, I had kids, I had an hour-and-a-half commute each way. But my deal was, 100% of the money I made from insurance was going into a separate bank account—and the only thing that came out of that was my lead expense. I didn't pay myself more; my personal bank account saw none of that money; I didn't pay off debt or credit cards, put my kids in a nice school, or buy a nice house or car. I did nothing differently.

My goal when I was part-time was to save six months of income—twenty thousand dollars at that point—and then quit my accounting job to go full-time into insurance.

So, if you come to me as a part-timer, I'm your guy; I started that way. The mistake I see a lot of people make is taking that extra eight hundred dollars from insurance work and spending it on a vacation or paying off a credit card. Is that your plan? Because if it is, it's going to be rough. You're going to be in the hamster wheel for a long time. In this industry, what you make this month will be different from the next. A client has to keep a policy for a year for you to get all of your money.

You have to make sure your expectations align properly with the work you are willing to take on. You only get out what you put in.

CHAPTER ELEVEN
SILK PAJAMAS

There's this quote that I never really had the need to pay attention to until somewhat recently in my life.

It's from boxing-hall-of-famer Marvelous Marvin Hagler. The middleweight great spent his childhood in Newark, New Jersey, along with his five siblings. He started boxing at age ten when a social worker introduced him to the sport. His parents struggled financially, and in 1967, at age fourteen, Hagler dropped out of school to work in a toy factory, helping to support the household.

That same year, violent protests swept through Newark, part of the "long, hot summer" of nationwide race riots during the Civil Rights Movement.

Hagler and his siblings spent more than three days on their bellies indoors, forbidden to stand, frequently retreating under their beds when bullets smashed through their apartment windows. After the violence subsided, his parents decided to relocate to Brockton, Massachusetts—around thirty-five miles south of Lynn, where I grew up.

Hagler recounted how the riots had a big impact on him. He described looking down from his high-rise apartment and seeing looters swarming the streets "like ants on a picnic table." Over a four-day period in July, 26 people were killed in the Newark riots, 727 were injured, and there was $10 million's worth of property damage.

Determined to make a better life for himself and spurred on by personal humiliation after losing a street fight, a then fifteen-year-old Hagler fully committed himself to training at a local boxing gym in Brockton.

Hagler would go on to become one of the greatest middleweight boxers of all time. He became the undisputed middleweight champion in 1980 and defended his titles twelve times over the next seven years, winning all but one of his defenses by knockout.

In 1988, Hagler lost his title to Sugar Ray Leonard in a controversial split decision that would prove to be Marvelous Marvin's final competitive bout. Hagler moved on to pursue an acting career shortly after the loss and never laced up the gloves again.

He initially campaigned for a rematch with Leonard, but when the chance eventually came his way in 1990 (along with a $15 million contract), he declined. When asked what had happened to his competitive zeal, Hagler delivered the killer quote:

"It's tough to get out of bed to do roadwork at 5:00 a.m. when you've been sleeping in silk pajamas."

Early on, Hagler had used his personal circumstances to drive him. He was a poor kid from a broken neighborhood: only his talent and work ethic were going to lift him out of his situation. And when he started to get to the upper echelons of boxing? No one was going to take his opportunity from him. Any time he thought about taking his foot off the gas—missing that early-morning run, skipping that sparring session—he thought about how his competitor would likely be training at that very second. No one was going to outwork him.

But what happens when it all works out? What happens when you win the titles you worked so hard for, you accrue the millions that you could only dream of as a kid? What happens when you reach the peak of the mountain top? What happens when there are no worlds left to conquer?

Hagler lost the motivation to compete with his peers. And at the top level, the margins are so slim that you need whatever edge you can create. He simply wasn't going to keep defeating hungry and determined opposition in that state of mind.

To me, Hagler is an inspiration when it comes to the power of grit and mental strength. He also proves how quickly that can all disappear when we become content.

When I look at my current lot in life and ask myself if I'm content, the short answer is: *hell no.*

I've achieved a lot, for sure. I'm rich. I've almost completed construction on my dream home. My wife and my children want for nothing. But the truth is, I'm just getting started.

If I'm Hagler, then growing and selling my business was my first title defense. There are plenty more to come. You see, I'm doing okay by the standards of the average person in my industry, but I'm nothing compared to the top dogs.

We are all human; we can all reach some level of complacency. Today, I don't grind at quite the level I used to when I was trying to make a name for myself as an agent. I have golf booked at 2:00 p.m. this Friday. I take nice vacations with my family. I certainly appreciate the fact that I don't have to slog away constantly and forgo any downtime. But don't get it twisted: I am as fiercely ambitious as I've ever been.

This is partly because I am conscious that it could all disappear tomorrow. I like to constantly challenge myself. Do you hate losing so much that you're willing to change? Or do you hate changing so much you are willing to lose?

The more money I make and the more success I have, the more I learn how little money I have and how little success I have.

Take Patrick Bet-David, who is a behemoth in the life insurance space. He sold his company to the same buyer I did, except he probably made thirty-times the money I did.

Bet-David offered political commentator Tucker Carlson $100 million to join his media company, and Carlson declined. Bet-David said he learned that day that he didn't have that much money, because he couldn't afford Tucker. A dude who sold his insurance company for $300 million is still seeing the bigger picture.

I've got guys who make $200,000 a year thinking they're king shit, that they're going to live forever. That kind of money goes away so quickly.

I live scared. I don't want to go back to being broke. I had a little taste of success in the mortgage business, and that went away quickly. So, I've spent the last ten years scared that this is all going to go away. I don't want to go backwards.

I don't think I've made it. I'm not in silk pajamas, metaphorical or otherwise. I don't think I've done that much.

I was at an event recently and someone asked me why I still work. I found that question so bizarre. What do you want me to do, sit at home all day eating Cheetos? I don't understand the alternative to what I'm doing.

I said to the guy, "I don't think I've accomplished shit yet."

"What do you mean? You're probably making forty times what I do."

And I was like, "Let me explain something to you."

The guy who owns Integrity Marketing Group, Bryan W. Adams, used to be an insurance agent just like me. Integrity acquired not only little old me, but also Patrick Bet-David and three hundred other partners.

My agency will do around $200 million in new premiums within a year. About fifteen thousand applications a month. Adams's company will do $23 billion this year. I am a rounding error in his world. I've done nothing. And Integrity is just one company; there are hundreds more.

I've done some cool stuff. I'm not confused. I am grateful, and I am happy. But I am not fully satisfied. If Bryan Adams isn't going to stop, why should I?

We have a lot of agents who go out and have a killer month, make fifty thousand dollars, and then won't work for two months. I'm like, *what?* I would want to keep adding to that $50,000 as much as possible in case it ever goes away.

I also want my kids to see that I've kept working. I've been lucky enough to help other people, so I'd want to continue doing that too. I feel like at this point, if I stop, it's not just me who potentially loses out.

It's so early in my career, and hopefully, so early in my life. I've seen some guys out there who have done some crazy, phenomenal things. Right now, I'm just a dude who lives in Kennesaw, Georgia. No one gives a shit about me outside of certain circles. I am just trying to be a bigger piece of the industry, a bigger piece of the world. If I stop right now, no one would give a crap. Bryan Adams ain't gonna slow down. Patrick Bet-David ain't gonna slow down.

I like achieving things. I like how that feels. And I like how the work I have done impacts other people—even outside my family.

In my company, if you issue $400,000 worth of premium a year, we consider you a "Hall of Fame" producer. Early on, my goal was to make as many Hall of Fame producers as I could. I'd been watching my colleague Marc Meade and noticed that he was really good at getting his producers to be Hall-of-Fame level. And that became a personal challenge of mine: to get more people on that level than he did. Marc didn't even know it at the time. But I thought that the number of people I could train to that level was a perfect reflection of my leadership. It's one thing if I do it, but can I help other people get to that place? That is a huge motivation.

And it's simple. I can tell any insurance agent in the country how to make $400,000. It's not that deep. I can lay out the steps for anyone. Here is how much you have to work, how many phone calls you have to make. Here are the numbers. Now, are you willing to do it?

Seeing how many Hall of Famers I could train became my new obsession. Now, it's almost obnoxious how many of them there are at my company.

I want to pull people up with me. I like seeing how my employee, Amanda, can support her twins and marriage on a six-figure salary. I was able to give her that opportunity instead of someone else because I worked my ass off. Man, I love that feeling.

For me, it's all been about setting new goals for myself. I've learned that people can often map out their goals quite poorly. Simply writing them down is a good start, but I don't think that's enough. People can write crap down on a piece of paper and look at it once in a blue moon or never again. I like to make it more of an active exercise. I break it into three columns.

GOALS	ADD	REMOVE
• Make 250k/year	• Book 30 Appointments/Week, 120/Month, 1500/Year	• Sleeping In
• Put kids in private school		• Watching Tv Nightly
• Buy wife a new house	• Be First At Office Dialing	• Flag Football
• Donate 5k to church	• Up @ 5am	• Stop Watching Football & Playing Fantasy Football
• Be the #1 producer in the agency	• Gym @ 5:30am	• Cut Out Alcohol
• Lose 25 pounds	• Automatic Lead Flow Weekly	

The left-hand column is for your goals. These can be financial; for example, one of my early goals was to put my kids through private school. Or it can be a wellbeing goal, like losing weight or focusing on your mental health.

The next column is a to-do list of actions you have to perform in order to make those goals happen. This step is too often missing for a lot of people when they plot out their aspirations. They don't provide themselves with practical footholds to make their goals more achievable. These actions can be about productivity or scheduling, like booking more appointments or arriving at work early.

And then there is the third column. This is the killer. It's a list of the stuff you have to give up to make it all happen. It's all the stuff you have to stop. Because there are only so many hours in the day. If you start something new, you have to give something else up. These are all your bad habits.

For me, it was stuff like sleeping in. I was addicted to sports and TV. I had a lot of hobbies that were useless. We all do dumb stuff. I drank vodka too much and too many times of the week, and that certainly didn't help.

Using the above method holds you accountable and increases your likelihood of keeping on track. Without this other stuff, a goal is just some vague shape in the distance. Now, it's something tangible. With this system, if you find yourself killing three hours a night on Netflix or SportsCenter, it'll hit you: "Oh wow, my kids are never getting to private school." If you're hitting snooze five times on your morning alarm, you're now reminded: "Crap, I'm not going to get that new house for my wife at this rate."

The consequences of your bad habits are readily apparent to you, and this makes them much harder to break.

Now, one of my new goals is to be relevant to Integrity Marketing Group, which is the company that acquired my agency. I went from being a big fish in a small pond to jumping in the ocean with the sharks at Integrity. My company might be issuing $200 million a year—while the mothership is hitting $25 billion—but I'm still a rounding error.

I'm about to embark on a major new challenge with this goal. I have to prove to the powers that be that I am a player, that I deserve a seat at the table. And in order to get there, I have to stop being complacent.

I am not going to lie; I've taken my foot off the gas somewhat with all this recent success. I go to the gym from 8:00 a.m. to 10:00 a.m. I drop my kid at school and hang out with him loads. It's great; I love it. But I've had my time to enjoy the fruits of my labor. It's time to park the cushy schedule and get back to grinding.

I want to be an important part of the machine. I was a big part of my company's machine, but at Integrity, there's three hundred partners, many of whom are more powerful than me in doing what I do. How do I stand out in that group?

When things first started taking off in my career, I remember telling my wife, "I think I'm at the top of all the bottom people."

A year later, it dawned on me, "I think I might be at the bottom of all the top people."

Now, it's like I've accessed a secret level, and man, I'm definitely at the bottom of this bitch. The more I make, the more I realize how little success I have relative to the real players.

I need to stop being complacent relative to that new level. Sometimes I take for granted what I've built. I get a lot of recognition for what I've done. I've established this agency to where it can grow if I show up to work or not. The business is growing. But I could for sure do more.

Which I've started to do. And I know that getting more involved in Integrity is going to put more on my plate. Because they are going to learn that I'm really good, and they are going to take advantage of that. They are going to say, "You are in charge of this now."

I like recognition. I can live without it, but I do like it. I've been recognized for standing out several times in my career. I'm at a company now that has a Partner of the Year prize. It's a stupid little trophy, but I'm not shy in saying I want that damn thing.

How do I get that? Right now, I'm not even in the running. I'm not even on the ballot. But I should be, because I have the ability. So, I need to do more for the company, more for my peers, more for the overall machine.

I like chasing things that seem hard. It's the same reason I ran my first marathon before I turned forty-seven and climbed giant mountains. I like chasing big, audacious, hard things. It keeps me focused. Me being focused is good. Being unfocused is a terrible thing for me and the people around me. I'm not enjoyable to be around; I sulk, I'm negative. But if I put my mind to something, I'm going to go and get it.

The goal is to have an infrastructure where I can provide services to the entire industry, so everyone can use the systems and automations that I use internally to build my agency. One of the things I have to do in order to achieve this goal is hire talented people, because I can only personally take it so far.

I've already designed the Do More Activity Tracker, which is available in spreadsheet form. The next step is working with my programmers to design an application and a web-based version.

I reached out to one of the corporate executives at Integrity with an idea, a concept that could help make recruiting for the whole company work better. I went through what we do for our team. And he said, "That might be the best thing that anyone's ever called me with. No one has brought that to my attention."

So now, me and my team are modeling that with him and seeing how it might apply to the wider organization. I will get paid on that eventually. But it won't be next week. It's all a big exercise in delayed gratification.

A lot of this is about being patient. I'm going through an insane period of delayed gratification following the acquisition of my company. If I figure out how to improve the internal mechanics of the parent company, it might not get me paid today, but man will I see a reward down the line. So, I have to continue to work my ass off, even if I don't see the immediate benefit today.

That's what people struggle with all the time, putting the effort in when the returns are far down the line. I preach this stuff, so now I have to walk the walk.

What makes it easier is taking the time to acknowledge that hard work when it all pays off. I recently attended the final Chapel Day before my daughter Gabby's graduation from private school, and you know what? I was a mess.

It just hit me all at once. All those monotonous hours working phones. All those early mornings, the endless miles on the road. The countless days coming home after sunset, the sleepless nights sick with worry, the hundreds and hundreds of canceled appointments and no-shows, the strain on my relationships.

And then I see my beautiful daughter attending her final days at the school I worked so hard to send her to. I became overwhelmed. Steph and Gabby were giggling at me, saying there must be a bunch of pollen in the air. I'm not that emotional of a dude.

I hope that some other kids get to go to private school and receive the best opportunities a comfortable upbringing has to offer, directly as a result of their parents reading this book. You can't put a value on that.

Oh, and any other goals? I really want a private jet. So, there's that. Like I said, I'm just getting started.

THE TOOLS YOU NEED

When it comes to the insurance space, about 90% of new agents quit within the first year, and 95% are gone within five years. You work under huge amounts of pressure to be successful, and if you don't see results straight away, it can be disheartening. Not only that, but the vast majority of agents don't feel supported.

That's why I've created a variety of tools and resources to help you on your journey. I believe in helping as many people as possible get everything they've ever wanted in life.

The first thing I recommend you do is visit my website johnwetmore.com, which will give you access to my weekly newsletter and personal activity tracker. Here's why I created it, and here's what you can expect:

- Skyrocketed my sales threefold
- Gave me crystal-clear insights into my time management
- Set me up with laser-focused objectives
- Boosted my sales effectiveness and return on investment
- Ensured I stayed on track, day in and day out
- Spotlights what I do best and where I can improve
- Empowered me to coach thousands of insurance pros to success
- Taught me to navigate sales with logic, cutting through the emotional clutter

You can also book one-on-one consultations with me through my website. My consultations are for:

- Insurance agencies looking to elevate their performance and achieve new milestones.

- Sales teams aiming to dominate the insurance market.

- Corporate groups seeking to enhance their insurance know-how and outcomes.

Each workshop is customized and tailored to match the unique goals and dynamics of your team.

I can also help revolutionize how your agency runs by transforming your business with automation. Insurance is an ever-evolving landscape; staying ahead requires innovation. I can assist with consulting and implementing automation services that can transform your operations.

Automation benefits most aspects of an agency, including lead distribution, agency tracking, recruiting, and follow-up.

I also travel the country, mentoring and speaking at events, so keep an eye out; I could be coming to your hometown soon.

For those of you that really want to commit and reach the next level, I invite you to fill out the form on my website and apply to join my team. Here's an overview of what you can expect:

- Training programs that are structured, proven to be effective, and absolutely free. You don't need prior experience in the world of insurance. You simply need to pay attention, ask questions, and have the motivation to push yourself harder than you ever thought possible.

- A lead program designed with innovation in mind, allowing each agent access to mortgage, final expense, term, IUL, and annuity leads.

- CRM (Customer Relationship Management) software that's cutting-edge, intuitive, and created to shave seconds off the clock. Among other features, our tracking system automatically uploads lead information into our system.

- Three possible income streams, including direct sales commissions, renewal commissions, and agency overrides.

- Compensation that's aggressive and intelligent.

- Pre-licensing costs paid in full if you're an unlicensed agent.

Subscribe to my YouTube channel for talks, tips, and trade insights. Follow me on Instagram, Facebook, and X for some unfiltered, straight-talking opinions on the insurance industry and succeeding in business in general.

If you'd like to take a further dive into how you can stop struggling and find your own potential I've designed a course to help you go from $0 to multi 6 figure income selling, where I have 20 videos and counting, even more tactical sales training and exercises that will empower you to immediately start seeing results. You can access here:

Finally, you can visit my website and gain access to my newly formulated coaching program, including personalized planning and unrivaled access to me and my training methods.

ACKNOWLEDGEMENTS

Without my wife Stephanie, none of this would have been possible. She has been there for me since the very beginning, back when I was broke, bankrupt, and living in an efficiency lodge. She was there not only to help raise the four kids I brought to the relationship but give us all a roof over our heads, help pay child support, and feed us, when I was struggling to do so.

I have had a lot to deal with in life, but Stephanie, you've stood by me and encouraged me during the hardest of times. I will always remember the times nobody else ever saw. Thank you for being the rock in my life that loves to give, loves to smile and is always a glass-half-full kind of person. You're an inspiration to me in so many ways and by far the strongest person

I have ever met. You are a complete badass and have handled more shit with a smile on your face than anyone I've ever known.

My assistant Amanda Bennett has—at the time of this writing—been with me for seven years (and is never allowed to leave LOL). She has been behind the scenes, building this company with me every step of the way since the day I hired her.

Amanda, I want to thank you for putting up with my crazy emotions, supporting many hard decisions in business, my crazy ideas (some that worked and many that didn't), and always being open to adapt and change everything we do. Without a complaint or hesitation, you've always had my back. We have also been through some very difficult times in business, so I appreciate you being willing to tell me when I'm acting like an idiot and need to look at things differently. There is nobody I've ever trusted more in business than you. Everything you've done to help agents, work with all of our staff over the years, handle all the business and life stuff I've thrown at you, just being exactly what I needed you to be along the way—I am forever grateful for that.

My mom has been a great inspiration to my life and business world. The biggest takeaway I've ever had came from her: that when you have a desire to get out of a crappy situation, you do whatever it takes to accomplish that goal.

Mom, I deserved every ass-whipping I've ever had with the dozens of paddles you used, including the indestructible one that still exists today. You had to be both Mom and Dad most of the time and I know that was an extremely hard role for you. You have always supported me being me and just let me fly, never questioning my decisions and yet always being there if I needed anything. Thanks for the foundation you built; without those moves you made to get us out of the hood, none of what I have today would have been possible.

To my amazing children, Shailey, TJ, Gabby, Brayden, and Maddox, I absolutely love all of you. Having children has been my favorite thing in life; as you all know, I love babies, so I just kept having more of you. My favorite memories are of you all enjoying your childhoods, playing games—usually in the dirt or puddles—and doing all the crazy things you always did. Whether there was any money or not, we always found a way to have fun and laugh.

I have messed up parenting a lot, many times over, especially as you've each aged. I've been impatient and stubborn and made poor choices in life that have affected all of you forever. With that, the one thing I've strived for in life is to do my absolute best to be a provider to all of you, and I appreciate you all for allowing me to sacrifice things, to accomplish my own personal dreams and goals of taking care of my family the best I can. I love watching you all become independent and build your own lives. I adore each one of you for your individual and unique personalities, and although you may not know it, every single day I worked in my life—even when I didn't want to—was driven by trying my best to not let any of you down and be an inspiration to whatever it is you dream to accomplish in this very short life we all get to live.

There are many, many mentors, partners, managers, and agents I've had the pleasure to learn from and work with in this business. Far too many to name them all, but I'd like to thank a very select few that have added more value to my life than I could ever explain in a book.

Mike Killimett for being there for me every step of the journey, teaching me patience, how to build an agency, and so much about communicating with people that I wouldn't be the same person today without that.

Marc Meade changed my sales career forever by laying out a path that any hard-working non-salesman could follow and achieve great success. You were such an inspiration to me; watching how hard you worked and kept this business so simple in my mind, and I could directly relate to how you aimed to help your family out of a financial situation. I appreciate you being such a great friend along the way. All the ups and downs we've been able to navigate together the last decade have forged a relationship unlike any other.

Shawn Meaike for taking insane chances in business that allowed me to have an opportunity like the one we've built. You've taught me so many lessons about communication, how to normalize and minimize things, and how to provide short-term goals and structure for others. You're one of a kind, and I appreciate you believing in me and allowing me to be me, even when things weren't so perfect.

There are many, many more of you, and I could write an entire book about all the people I've been fortunate enough to cross paths with, who have helped me accomplish things I sometimes get far too much credit for. Thank you to everyone along the way—even the haters—as you've all fueled me to do more.

I'm looking forward to the next chapters of life and business with many more of you!

www.ingramcontent.com/pod-product-compliance
Lightning Source LLC
Chambersburg PA
CBHW061639040426
42446CB00010B/1499